FAITH LISTENING

A | Awaken to God's Life
B | Bless God's Name
C | Celebrate God's Presence

Jo Anne Grace, Ph.D.

WestBow Press books may be ordered through booksellers or by contacting:

WestBow Press
A Division of Thomas Nelson & Zondervan
1663 Liberty Drive
Bloomington, IN 47403
www.westbowpress.com
844-714-3454

ISBN: 978-1-6642-8707-5 (sc)
ISBN: 978-1-6642-8708-2 (e)

Library of Congress Control Number: 2022923297

Print information available on the last page.

WestBow Press rev. date: 10/18/2023

WESTBOW
PRESS®
A DIVISION OF THOMAS NELSON
& ZONDERVAN

This book is dedicated to the Glory of God as revealed through family, friends, and clients. They have taught me that God can do infinitely more than we can ask or imagine. May it be so for you as you as you journey through the pages of this book.

CONTENTS

. . . .

INTRODUCTION | Connecting with God

· ·

"Be reconciled to God"

—2 Corinthians 5:20

Faith Listening connects you with God. God is actively present in the world today. Whether in times of joy or sadness and in times of trauma or celebration, God is there. Faith Listening links the reality of human life with the certainty of God's Life-Giving Spirit. By following a basic ABC pattern of discernment, you will know Who God is and How God is acting in your life.

What is discernment except the embrace of God acting in and through creation?[1] Discernment is an active process in which a person tunes into the Mystery of God at work. It calls upon wonderment and imagination. Faith Listening is a discernment skill that opens a door to respond to God's Action. It provides an avenue to respond soulfully to God, rather than reacting solely to humans. It does not change the fact that something has happened, but rather it invites a new creation and a new meaning.

Faith Listening asks that we bring our human stories into the reflective light of the revelation of God from Genesis to Revelation. It takes seriously Paul's mandate, "Be reconciled to God!"

> From now on, therefore, we regard no one from a human point of view, even though we once knew Christ from a human point of view. So, if anyone is in Christ, there is a new creation, everything old has passed away, see, everything has become new! All this is from God, who reconciled us to himself through Christ, and has given us the ministry of reconciliation. So, we are ambassadors for Christ, since God is making his appeal through us, we entreat you on behalf of Christ, be reconciled to God (2 Corinthians 5:16–20).

I met with Tom, age thirty-eight, who was injured on the job and complained of chronic back pain. Although his pain was high and his medication offered some relief, his suffering was greater. In the past, he found comfort by going to church. Tom told me, "But now, when I walk into a church, all I see is the cross." Then, he said, "I know the cross represents Jesus, His agony and passion, and Jesus points to God who is his Father, but all I see is my father who is cross. His angry words at the dinner table and his rage still flood my body after all these years. I cannot seem to get over it. I feel cut off from God." Listening to his story through the ears of faith, in which God is the subject, I asked him, "What is your greatest need?" Tom thought for a moment, let out a sigh, and replied, "Comfort!" I said, "Isn't God the Comforter?" He said, "Yes, the Comforter is the Holy Spirit!" Then, together we brainstormed other stories about God Who comforted His

1

people. Tom took a deep, relaxing breath when he heard Jesus's words: "And I will pray to the Father, and he shall give you another Comforter, that he may abide with you forever" (John 14:16). Somewhere deep inside, a change occurred. Only Tom could explain it when he was ready. So, I asked him to continue breathing in and out while saying to himself a simple Breath Prayer: "Blessed be God, The Comforter." We sat in quiet reflection while each of us prayed inwardly the Breath Prayer. Tom focused on God and experienced the reality of being reconciled to a God he could grasp amidst his suffering.

This is just one of the many stories you will read that demonstrate the practicality of Faith Listening. Faith Listening is a learned skill. Its purpose is to discern Who God is and What God is doing in the context of human stories. In its simplest form, it identifies the human need and makes a connection to God who "supplies our every need" (Philippians 4:19-20). In its more complex form, physical pain, emotional anguish, mental distress, behavioral trouble, or spiritual suffering points to the dynamic pneumasomatic[2] action of integrating God's Life with human experiences and relationships.

Perhaps you noticed that the ancient spiritual practice of blessing God was used as a Breath Prayer in Tom's case above. Faith Listening encourages the use of a Blessing Prayer and the extension of a Blessing Litany as a prayer of adoration, an alternative prayer form to petition and intercession. Matilda states in her story, found in Chapter 1, "Now I don't have to worry! I guess we both needed the God of Peace. This Blessing Prayer … it is like petition and intercession rolled into one."

Faith Listening was developed at the request of health professionals who wanted to learn how to integrate health and spirituality. Those who are in physical pain and spiritual distress have benefited from practicing Faith Listening. It was further refined when pastors and pastoral counselors wanted to know how to encourage wholeness of body, soul, and spirit. Those who are emotionally upset, mentally suffering, or behaviorally trapped have found reconciliation and healing. Over the course of the past forty years, many who wanted a closer walk with God or who asked, "Where is God? Why me?" have experienced a deeper relationship and been reunited with God. Practically speaking, the ability to hear with the ears of faith has been beneficial to those who have lost their faith or have no faith.

What is faith except the Mystery of God at work? Faith is the "assurance of things hoped for, the conviction of things unseen" (Hebrews 11). Faith is a response to God who is the subject of faith. Faith bears witness to the fact that the unseen reality of God is ever present in the human condition of experiences and relationships. "Have not I commanded thee? Be strong and of a good courage; be not afraid, neither be thou dismayed: for the LORD thy God is with thee wherever you go" (Joshua 1:9).

When we listen to stories with the ears of faith, we hear Who God is and What God is doing. This shines through the human drama of everyday life.

Discerning God's Presence is a natural way of perceiving world events and human experiences, if we keep three theological presuppositions in mind: covenant, formation, and body.

First, Covenant Theology[3] informs all relationships because God makes covenant with all creation throughout all time. God is The Creator, and we are the creatures. Second, Formation Theology[4] recognizes that God formed humankind in God's image, male and female, and it was good. It encourages praising God: for we are fearfully and wonderfully made. Marvelous are God's works. Third, Body Theology[5] embraces the reality that the body is the place wherein God resides. "Do you not know that you are a temple of God and the Holy Spirit dwells within you?" (1 Corinthians 3:16).

Faith Listening follows a basic ABC pattern: A| Awaken to God's Life, B | Bless God's Name, C |Celebrate God's Presence. First, awaken to God's Life. All too often we remember who did what to whom, rather than remembering Who God is and How God acts. We practice amnesia, forgetting God, rather than anamnēsis,[6] remembering God. Second, bless God's Name. This ancient spiritual practice honors God. It recognizes that God acts in and through creation. It is one way to pray without ceasing.[7] Third, celebrate God's Presence. This celebration finds its expression in words, thoughts, and actions. By remaining in God's Presence, we can hear God's Call, open ourselves to God's Spirit, and act in God's Service to others.

This book provides a framework for discerning God's Presence. You can apply the ABC pattern to any relationship, experience, or event in your life. If you are caught in conflict or confusion, go to Chapter 1| The Body/Person and the Simplicity of Need. If your physical pain consumes you, go to Chapter 2| The Body/ Physical and the Signal of Pain. If you are stuck in traumatic memories or critical judgments, go to Chapter 3| The Body/Mental and the Capacity of the Mind. If you are experiencing emotional distress, go to Chapter 4| The Body/Emotional and the Purpose of Emotions. If you are dealing with destructive behaviors, go to Chapter 5| The Body/Behavioral and the Intent of Behaviors. If you are suffering from spiritual dryness or distressing dreams, go to Chapter 6| The Body/Spiritual and the Symbol of Dreams.

An overview of how Faith Listening works is best understood by using a case study. Susan, age fifty-four, complained of chronic tension in her *neck* and across her shoulders. She was *caught* in a relationship that caused her great *anxiety*. Susan found herself getting angry and *throwing books* across the room. When I asked her, "What is your greatest need?" Susan replied, "I need to sit down and find peace and quiet." Gradually, she discerned Who God is and How God is actively present in her life.

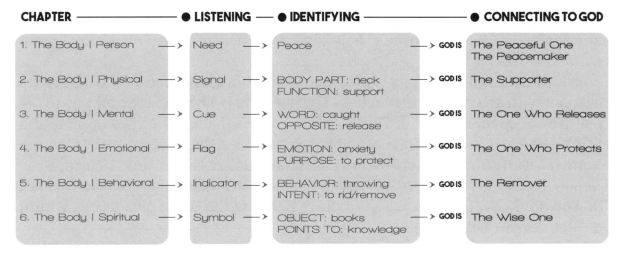

CHAPTER	● LISTENING	● IDENTIFYING	● CONNECTING TO GOD
1. The Body | Person	Need	Peace	GOD IS The Peaceful One / The Peacemaker
2. The Body | Physical	Signal	BODY PART: neck / FUNCTION: support	GOD IS The Supporter
3. The Body | Mental	Cue	WORD: caught / OPPOSITE: release	GOD IS The One Who Releases
4. The Body | Emotional	Flag	EMOTION: anxiety / PURPOSE: to protect	GOD IS The One Who Protects
5. The Body | Behavioral	Indicator	BEHAVIOR: throwing / INTENT: to rid/remove	GOD IS The Remover
6. The Body | Spiritual	Symbol	OBJECT: books / POINTS TO: knowledge	GOD IS The Wise One

Susan's ABC practice of Faith Listening led her to create a Blessing Litany.

Susan's Blessing Litany

Blessed are You, LORD God, **The Peaceful One.**
Blessed are You, LORD God, **The Peace Maker.**
Blessed are You, LORD God, **The Giver of Peace.**
Blessed be God, **The Protector.**
Blessed be God, **The One Who is Perfect Love.**
Blessed be God, **The One Who Casts Out All Fear.**
Blessed be God, **The One Who Removes.**
Blessed are You, **The Releaser.**
Blessed are You, **The Wise One.**

If all this seems overwhelming or difficult to grasp, be patient. Keep it simple. Start with Chapter 1. Read each chapter and use the practical guide at the end of the chapter to increase your Faith Listening skills. Some have said, "This is like learning a new language." Others have said, "Now I know what it means to let go and let God!" This book encourages you to connect with God by identifying your physical signals, mental cues, emotional flags, behavioral indicators, and spiritual symbols. Just like Susan, you will experience God's Power of reconciling and healing when you practice the ABCs of Faith Listening.

Faith Listening does not change the fact that an experience occurred or that a relationship existed. It does change a person's response to an experience or relationship in such a way that God's Presence shines through to integrate physical reality with spiritual certainty. The key to Faith Listening is to know that the subject of faith is God. Your objective is to remember God when you recall your life experiences or hear other people tell their stories. Sometimes, it will make no sense to you because it is about God's relationship with the other person. Other times, it will make perfect sense to you because it provides new insights into the Character and Nature of God at work in and among us.

May you find through the pages of this book an awakening, a blessing, and a celebration of God's Life within you!

CHAPTER 1 | The Body/Whole and the Simplicity of Need

. . . .

May God supply all your needs according to His riches in Glory by Jesus
Christ. Now unto God and our Father be the glory forever and ever. Amen!
—Philippians 4:19-20

It is an amazing experience to unwrap the gift of reconciliation as it occurs while listening through the ears of faith. Whether you apply Faith Listening to your own story or those of others, the riches of being in God's Presence are awe-inspiring. No longer absorbed by human points of view, we are bathed by the light of God creating anew. From the simplicity of need to the discovery of How God supplies every need, we are free to settle into a safe place. It is in this place that the "still small voice" (1 Kings 19:12) resounds with new insights and meaning.

Let us begin to explore the discernment skill of Faith Listening from the perspective of need. Upon completion of this chapter, you will practice identifying your need, naming God, and grasping the basic ABCs of Faith Listening.

> A | Awaken to God's Life
> B | Bless God's Name
> C | Celebrate God's Presence

A | AWAKEN TO GOD'S LIFE

Most of us awaken to an alarm, setting the tone of the day: hurry up! Some of us have the luxury of awakening slowly, but we are immediately consumed by our to-do lists: who does what by when? Few of us awaken anticipating God's Life at work in and among us. Yet, God is The Present One.

A little child knows how to awaken to God's Life. It is an effortless response to daily living, but it is all too quickly forgotten. For example, a four-year-old girl knows she is going to have a baby brother. Her parents have been preparing her for the exciting event. Each evening at dinner, the conversation is punctuated by her constant inquiry: "Yes, but when will I get to be alone with my baby brother?" After seven days of hearing the same question, her parents promise her, "After your baby brother comes home from the hospital, you can be alone with him." The little girl is excited. That very night her baby brother is born.

Several days later, it is time to bring the baby home. The little girl gets to help hold, feed, and wash him. But, not once does she get to be alone with him. So, she begins to question her parents again. "When do I get to be alone with my baby brother?" The parents have not forgotten about her request. They are simply paralyzed with fear. All the reading they have done about sibling rivalry has prepared them for the worst that can happen at this age when one child is jealous of another.

Another week goes by as the parents wrestle with their own fears. The little girl is becoming increasingly anxious to be alone with her brother. They know they must do something. One evening during dinner, the baby monitor is turned on. They hear the baby awaken from a late nap. The parents smile at each other. They look at their daughter and say, "Tonight's the night!" The little girl is filled with joy.

Bedtime draws near. They tuck the baby into his crib. Together, they read a bedtime story. The father tells the little girl after the story is finished, "Now is the time!" The parents leave, close the door, and listen outside the room with the baby monitor in hand.

This is what they hear. At first there is nothing but silence. The little girl has waited so long for this moment that she is awed and speechless. But then, after she looks around the room to be sure she is alone with her baby brother, she whispers with urgency, "Quick! Before I forget, tell me about God." The brother coos, and the sister smiles.

Amnesia, meaning *to forget*, is the spiritual antithesis of anamnēsis, meaning *to remember*. The little girl was awakened to God's Life. She knew her little brother was with God. She knew innately that where life is, God is near. God is present. Some of us, like the little girl, take steps to keep alive the memory that God and life are one. Others of us gradually forget and come down with severe cases of amnesia. We become very good at remembering who did what to whom, when, and where, without any mention of God. The life we experience, the stories we tell, and even the scripture we read lack the benefit of a faith perspective.

A faith perspective is one in which God is remembered. God is the subject of faith. We are the responders. Without God, we merely react. Faith Listening encourages us to respond to God. It begins when we awaken to God's Life. This can best be understood by recalling the Israelites traveling in the wilderness. They were forgetting God constantly and wanting to return to Egypt with every hardship they endured. But, Moses identified their needs and turned to God on their behalf. The result was an immediate response from God to satisfy their needs: thirst, hunger, and homeland.

God is with us! The Israelites had to be reminded of this fact repeatedly during their forty-year sojourn in the wilderness (Exodus 15:22-27). First, Moses led the Israelites out of the Red Sea into the wilderness of Shur. Three days later, they found water at Marah, but it was bitter. The people complained against Moses, and Moses cried out to God. God showed him a piece of wood, Moses threw it into the water, and the water became sweet. God satisfied their thirst. God promised not to inflict any diseases upon them that He did to the Egyptians, if they would listen to His voice, do what was right, and keep His commandments: for "I am the LORD who heals." They continued to Elam and camped where there were twelve springs of water and seventy palm trees.

Second, Moses set out from Elam into the Wilderness of Sin (Exodus 16:1-36). Here the people complained again, wanting to return to Egypt where they could fill their bellies and be satisfied. Moses turned to God, who heard their complaint. God responded to their need for food by raining manna (bread) from heaven in the morning and providing quails in the evening. Specific instructions were given to harvest the mana and gather the quail over seven days. They continued in this way for forty years, satisfying their needs with God's provisions and keeping God's commandments, including keeping Sabbath on the seventh day.

Third, the people journeyed by stages to the land God promised to give them (Exodus 17:1-7). But, they forgot the fact that God provided for their needs at each stage. When their needs consumed them, they complained to Moses. Once again, they begged for water. Moses asked, "Why do you quarrel with me? Why do you test God?" He told them that their complaint was not against him but against God. Moses turned to God, wondering what he should do because he was about to be stoned by the people. God instructed Moses to go ahead of the people, to take some of the elders with him, to take the staff with which he used to strike the Red Sea, and to go to Horeb. God said He would be standing in front of Moses on the rock at Horeb. He told Moses to strike the rock in front of the elders. When Moses did so, the waters flowed out for the people to drink. Moses called this place Massah, meaning *to quarrel*, and Meribah, meaning *to test*. This was to satisfy the Israelites' question: "Is the LORD among us or not?"

And so continues the human saga of forgetting God—amnesia—and remembering God—anamnēsis. There is a dynamic connection between the human drama unfolding before our very eyes and the Story of God's Life being disclosed in our everyday experience. It is a paradox when human need consumes our ever-growing experience of God living in and among us. Human need compels a response from God, who is revealed in a new light. As we awaken to God's Life, we are swept up into blessing God's Name and celebrating God's Presence.

B | BLESS GOD'S NAME

¹ Bless the LORD, O my soul; and all that is within me, bless God's holy name!

² Bless the LORD, O my soul, and forget not all his benefits

³ who forgives all your iniquity, who heals all your diseases,

⁴ who redeems your life from the Pit, who crowns you with steadfast love and mercy,

⁵ who satisfies you with good as long as you live so that your youth is renewed like the eagles (Psalm 103).

This psalm is one example of many that point to the spiritual tradition of blessing God's Name.[8] This tradition is common among Jewish people at greetings and departures. They bless God on special occasions, such as weddings and funerals, and at life's climactic moments, both good and bad. Christians say it in the form of a benediction. For example, "May God bless you with peace!" It can be heard in our common language. For example, when someone sneezes, some say, "God bless you!" This ancient spiritual practice of blessing is an essential component of Faith Listening.

The purpose of a blessing is to acknowledge that God is to be adored and remembered in all things. All too often, God's Name is obscured by the trauma of an event or the passion of a relationship. My needs, my desires, or my emotions overwhelm God's Action for life. It is easier to become obsessed with another person or myself, rather than be consumed by the dynamic Presence of God, Who is The Other. It takes a discerning ear to bless God's Name in the face of daily life experiences. It takes a familiarity with How God is named to celebrate God's Presence.

Most of us are familiar with a few Names for God. Yet, each of the monotheistic traditions record a Name for God based on God's Attribute or Character.[9] Christians recognize different Names as revealed in the Bible from Genesis to Revelation.[10] Muslims count ninety-nine Names for God found in the Koran.[11] The development of naming the One God with many Names originates in the Torah. Jews believed that the Name G_d was too holy and sacred to be pronounced. Instead, they called God Yahweh.[12]

This trend to name God continued as people encountered God in the common experiences of everyday life. Often, a Name for God was given based on God's Action. For example, Hagar was sent into the wilderness by Sarai where she encounters a messenger of God giving her instructions. "So, she named the LORD who spoke to her, 'You are El-Roi, The One Who Sees.'" For she said, "Have I really seen God and remained alive after seeing him?" (Genesis 16:7-15).

Even children and places are named after God's Action.[13] Hagar named her son Ismael, meaning *God hears.* Joseph named his firstborn Manasseh: "for God has made me forget all my hardship and all my father's house" (Genesis 41:51). He named his second born Ephraim: "for God has made me fruitful in the land of my misfortunes" (Genesis 41:52).

Moses is introduced to God's Name when he inquires, "If I come to the Israelites and say to them, 'The God of your ancestors has sent me to you,' and they ask me, 'What is his name? What shall I say to them?' God said to Moses, 'I AM WHO I AM.' God said further, 'Thus you shall say to the Israelites, I AM has sent me to you.' God also said to Moses, 'Thus you shall say to the Israelites, The LORD, the God of Abraham, the God of Isaac, and the God of Jacob has sent me to you. This is my name forever, and this my title for all generations'" (Exodus 3:13-15).

This passage provides insight into discerning God's Name. In this example, God's Being, "I AM," and God's Doing, "has sent," give rise to a Name for God. God is The One Who Sends. The evolution of God's Name continues to be revealed in scripture through common language with the basic premise that God is what

God does. Jesus refers to God as The Father, a familiar reference to The Creator God. Like a parent, God is in an intimate relationship with humankind. Jesus adopts the tradition of naming God through the unspoken backdrop of God's Name which is The Great "I AM." This is seen clearly when Jesus says, "I am the light of the world" (John 8:12), "I am the bread of life" (John 6:35), and "I am the good shepherd (John 10:14).

Faith Listening centers itself in the spiritual tradition of naming God as described in the Hebrew and Christian Bibles. It presupposes that God is named and remembered in light of the unfolding drama of human experiences and relationships. God's Name may be a title: Creator, King, or Judge. It may refer to God's Character: love, peace, or good. It may even describe God's Nature: jealous, consuming fire, or spirit. Whether title, character, or nature, a manifestation of God's Presence is implied in naming God. In other words, God's Name presupposes God's Presence. And, it is believed that the beneficial power of God's Presence is increased by blessing God's Name.

Faith Listening cultivates the spiritual tradition of blessing God's Name as found throughout scripture. The most common blessing form begins with "Blessed be God" and continues with God's Name or title with a corresponding action. One example is "Blessed be God, King of the Universe, who brings forth bread and wine." Blessings can also be spoken where humans are the object of a divine blessing. For example, "May the God of hope fill you with all joy and peace in believing" (Romans 15:13a).

Practically speaking, it is easy to move from human need to God who supplies that need. Moses demonstrates this when he takes each need to God, names God, and blesses God. Moses could not conceive of life without God's Presence no matter the circumstances. Since needs often come in numbers, it is possible to list them and create a Blessing Litany. Earlier, we talked about the Israelites traveling through the dessert. Each time they grumbled, Moses identified a need. Each time Moses identified a need, he named God. He even named his children to acknowledge and honor God. For example, Moses named his children, Gershom, meaning *a stranger there* (Exodus 2:22) and Eliezer, meaning *God is my help* (Exodus 18.4). This suggests that God is with us.[14] Each time Moses named God, he celebrated God's Presence amidst his human condition.

If Moses created a Blessing Litany, it might read as follows:

> **Moses' Blessing Litany**
>
> Blessed are You, LORD God, **The One Who Heals.**
> Blessed be God, **The Healer.**
> Blessed are You, LORD God, **The One Who Satisfies.**
> Blessed be God, **The Satisfier.**
> Blessed are You, LORD God, **The One Who Provides.**
> Blessed be God, **The Provider.**
> Blessed are You, LORD God, **The One Who Quarrels.**
> Blessed be God, **The Quarreler.**
> Blessed are You, LORD God, **The One Who Tests.**
> Blessed be God, **The Tester.**
> Blessed are You, LORD God, **The One Who is There.**
> Blessed be God, **The Stranger.**
> Blessed are You, LORD God, **The One Who Helps.**
> Blessed be God, **The Helper.**
> Blessed are You, LORD God, **The Great I AM.**
> Blessed be God, **The Great I AM.**

C | CELEBRATE GOD'S PRESENCE

Celebrating God's Presence, after awakening to God's Life and blessing God's Name, is a natural progression of Faith Listening. Just as the written text of scripture awakens us to the Story of God's Life, so too, the living text of a person's story blesses God's Name. As these steps of Faith Listening are applied to the human drama of life, God's Presence is celebrated. This celebration finds its expression in word, thought, and action. First, words are given, and Faith Listening is activated. Second, thoughts are formed, and faith reasoning is stimulated. Third, actions are taken, and faith expressions are realized.

The possibility of celebrating God's Presence occurs each time a journal entry is made or a story is told. For example, Matilda, age fifty-eight, came to see me with a desire for spiritual direction specific to a change in her career and marital status. She was concerned about starting a new business and retiring from an office position she had held for eighteen years. In addition, she and her husband were separated after thirty-five years of marriage, and it appeared that a divorce was imminent. She described her family system as dysfunctional with issues of alcoholism and abuse at its core. Despite her presenting issues and identified new opportunities, all conversation centered on her grandson, Alex.

Alex is a teenager, age fourteen, who in her words "has been hardest hit by family events. He is filled with rage and anger. He has begun acting out. His grades in school have slipped below his standard of A and B." Alex is close to his grandmother. She offers a stabilizing influence in his life that his parents have been unable to provide. Matilda is at her wits end because she feels that as a grandmother there should be something she can do. The more she talked, the more I became aware that she was consumed by her anxiety over the pain in her grandson and by her inability to take any creative action on his behalf.

As she told her story, Faith Listening became activated in me. The key words I heard punctuated were *rage* and *anger*. Faith reasoning was stimulated as thoughts begin to form and I listened. The variety of God's Names that were associated with *rage* and *anger* such as The Jealous One, The Angry One, and The Vengeful One did not seem to fit. There seemed to be no direct correlation between the Action and a Name for God in this situation. Yet, I remained curious. Who was the God most needed in this situation? I did not have a clue. So, I asked Matilda to identify what she thought Alex needed most in his current situation. I asked her, "What is missing in his life that would make a difference for him?" Immediately, she said, "Peace." Here was a Name for God that we could both grasp. God is Peace.

Since Matilda had already identified a great need to act, I suggested she use a Blessing Prayer as a simple faith expression. First, I asked her to say a Blessing Prayer by inhaling to the words "Blessed are You, LORD God," and exhaling to God's Name, The One Who Brings Peace. Second, after she celebrated God's Presence by repeating the Blessing Prayer to herself silently, I asked her to say a Blessing Prayer for her grandson, Alex. She added the words, "May God, Who is Peace, bless Alex." After several silent inhalations and exhalations, a great grin spread across her face. She said, "Now, I don't have to worry. I guess we both needed the God of Peace. This Blessing Prayer … it's like petition and intercession rolled into one."

After reading many examples of how to convert a need into a Name for God, it is time for you to create your own Blessing Litany and find your own Blessing Prayer. Discover how your needs lead you into God's Presence by following the instructions in Practice Guide| Chapter 1| The Body/Whole and the Simplicity of Need.

May God, The Supplying One, fulfill your every need!

It is time to apply Faith Listening to your story. What is your story or complaint? Write a few sentences about a current situation or a relationship. It might be an experience that consumes you. Maybe every time you turn around you think about it. It may be a relationship that pushes your buttons. Maybe you react by doing the things you do not want to do and by not doing the things you do want to do. Write down your story.

_____

_____

_____

_____

A | Awaken to God's Life

Let Faith Listening activate your words. Set the content of your life's story into the context of God's Life. Begin by taking a few deep breaths. Listen carefully through your story to your needs. Ask yourself, "What do I need?" Make a list.

Needs List _____

_____

_____

B | Bless God's Name

Translate your need into a Name for God. If your need is peace, then God is The Peacemaker, The Peaceful One. Remember: God supplies our every need!

Need   **God's Name**

_____ God is _____

_____ God is _____

_____ God is _____

C | Celebrate God's Presence

There are three ways to come into God's Presence. All draw on the ancient spiritual practice of blessing God. First, create your Blessing Litany. Second, read your Blessing Litany. Third, establish your Blessing Prayer which is a prayer of adoration.

Create a Blessing Litany

Transfer the Names of God that you discovered in section B | Bless God's Name. Each one is a Blessing Statement within your litany.

Blessing Litany

Blessed are You, LORD God, _____

Blessed are You, LORD God, _____

Blessed are You, LORD God, _____

② Read your Blessing Litany

Say your Blessing Litany aloud. Inhale when you say "Blessed are You, LORD God," and exhale to "God's Name" for each Blessing Statement.

Repeat your Blessing Litany silently to yourself. Say your Blessing Prayer in rhythm to your breath.

③ Establish your Blessing Prayer

Choose one Blessing Statement from your Blessing Litany that captures your attention or imagination.

Select one that deepens your breath or relaxes your muscles. Pick one that you like best or makes the most sense to you. Open yourself to the reality that God's Spirit, Pneuma, is with every breath you take. Remember: God is Life. Life is Breath. Breath is God.

> **Blessing Prayer**
>
> _____

Breathe your Blessing Prayer, a Prayer of Adoration, through your body. Repeat this prayer three times. Inhale when you say, "Blessed are You, LORD God," and exhale to "God's Name."

Reflect on Your Story

? What difference does it make when you apply Faith Listening to the Body/Person and the Simplicity of Need?

? What happens when you let God supply your every need?

? Did you notice any changes in your breathing or in your muscles?

? What is it like to discern God's Presence with you?

? What new insights or discoveries have you made?

Other Faith Listening Opportunities

☐ Brainstorm a list of needs. Write them down. Convert each need into a Name for God. For example, if the need is security, then God's Name is The Secure One.

☐ Choose a friend's story. Ask the person to share a story or use one that he/she has told you often. Make sure to ask the person what they need. Apply the ABCs of Faith Listening to his/her story.

CHAPTER 2 | The Body/Physical and the Signal of Pain

. . . .

Do you not know you are the temple of the Holy Spirit,
and the Spirit of God dwells within you?
—1 Corinthians 3:16

What is the body/physical except the place wherein God resides? The land in which God dwells encompasses not only the wide-open spaces where His people live, but also the interior landscape of the whole person. This intimate relationship with a Creator God from the beginning in the Garden of Eden to the travels with a Covenant God into Jerusalem and beyond remained alive in a communal body of people. During this sojourn, God is located first in the Ark of the Covenant, second in the Tent, third in the Temple, and finally in the Body of Christ.

Along the way, Jesus, Who is The Head of The Body, leads us to the Heart of God's Life in the personal life of each human being. Just as before, God finds a dwelling place. Jesus shows us that it is not only in the communal body, but also in a personal body. In Hebrew, the personal body is the whole person. There is no separation of body, soul, and spirit. There is no understanding of a bodily existence, being human, without God. God is Life. Life is Breath. Breath is God. In other words, without God, without Breath, pain arises.

What is pain except a signal for life? Pain functions as a protection system designed biologically to warn of danger. Danger is both a crisis and an opportunity. The crisis exists when healing resources are not brought to bear at the site of the injury or pain. If you have ever suffered a serious cut, and the blood is not stopped, you may bleed to death. The opportunity exists when we grasp that pain is a crossroad between life and death. God is The Giver of Life and Death. Pain is a sign of the Mystery of God acting in and through creation.

Paul speaks of all creation groaning and travailing in pain together until now.[15] Although we live in the flesh, in the body/physical, God's Spirit dwells in us. Let us be clear! Physical pain is the body's cry for life. We cannot deny the reality of pain, both physically and spiritually. Physically, it is wise to have any persistent pain signals checked by a qualified medical doctor. Spiritually, it is wise to know God specific to the signal of pain crying out for life.

Job realizes that there are two ways to know God. "God speaks in one way and in two though people do not perceive it. In a dream, in a vision of the night … and in pain" (Job 33:14-20). Much has been written about dreams and their interpretation based on a psychological perspective. A theological perspective on dreams is offered in Chapter 6. But, for now, it is time to explore an interpretive grid for pain based on a theological perspective.[16] Whether it is the pain of birth, the pain of devastation, or the pain of injury, life springs anew when we, like Job, remember God's Name and bless God for Who God is and What God is doing.

Upon completion of the chapter, you will practice the ABCs of Faith Listening by focusing on pain in the body/physical. You will discover "physical words pregnant with theological meaning."[17] You will explore how the physical function of a body part gives way to God's Name. You will learn how to listen to the voice of pain by using its signal to remind you of God's Presence. Let us turn our attention to the body/physical and the signal of pain.

A | AWAKEN TO GOD'S LIFE

Pain is a paradox. It is a mystery or a puzzle to be understood. Pain is a biological indicator of life and a theological guide to God's Life. Both are attempts to understand pain from different perspectives. On the one hand, biological or physiological inquiry depends upon empirical or measurable evidence. On the other hand, theological or spiritual inquiry depends on heuristic or exploratory experience. Both operate in the realm of a concrete and a tangible world. In either case, pain, as a signal, offers the opportunity to awaken to the miracle of life springing forth anew.

Physiologically speaking, pain is experienced in the mind. Pain receptors trigger a reflexive action. They are sensory based and widely spread throughout the skin and internal tissues except those in the brain. When any tissue is damaged, a warning signal goes off, and the protective function of pain goes into action. If we fail to heed the warning sign, such as a headache, or if pain receptors cease to trigger a neurological signal, such as in leprosy, permanent damage occurs. If we listen, healing resources are activated, tissues are repaired, and the body/physical becomes fully functional.

Theologically speaking, pain is a marker of the Presence of God. Pain indicates a state of being separated from God. This condition is referred to as sin. But, if pain is understood only as a consequence of sin or a punishment from God, it is misguided. It fails to embrace the incarnational reality of a Living God expressed through the life, death, and resurrection of Jesus. When pain is grasped as a reminder of a Covenant God who lives in intimate relationship with a body of people and each human being, then pain becomes a communication signal with the intent of being reconciled to God Who is Ever-Present. No longer do we cry out, "What have I done? Why am I being punished? Where is God?" Rather, we engage our imagination and wonder, "Who is God? How is God present?"

Peter, age forty-two, is an Anglo American. Peter wanted "to get a handle on his physical pain and integrate his spiritual life." He told me, "It started with a strange episode and was diagnosed as multiple sclerosis. Usually MS is not painful, but mine is. I have pain that starts in my lower back and moves both up into my neck and down into my legs in a shooting pain. The pain radiates into my arms, and I have headaches daily. Basically, pain is all over my body. It is a cry of triumph … let us see how much we can pile on and where the breaking point is … a disease like this and pain like this is a monster that rages inside." Together, we embarked upon a spiritual journey to discern God's Presence in a way that Peter could understand by using his pain as a guide. Upon completion, Peter gave voice to his pain. He said, "It is a cry of victory. It is a cry from God for my heart."

Peter awakened to God's Life dwelling within him. Peter's pain decreased, his senses became aware of God, and his movement followed God's Call for his life. I met Peter several years later when our paths crossed again at a conference. He had moved from his wheelchair to walking with God through an active ministry as a deacon. Peter is an example of integrating a theological perspective of pain with a medical perspective. First, he located himself in scripture. Second, he found biological words pregnant with theological meaning. And third, he identified the function of each biological word specific to God's Name. With each step, he learned to discern God's Presence and to bless God for Who God is and What God is doing.

B | BLESS GOD'S NAME

Let us take a closer look at the steps Peter took to bless God's Name. They are: locate, find, and identify. First, locate your story of pain into the context of God's Life as revealed in scripture from Genesis to Revelation. Second, find words that offer a range of meaning, connecting biological words with theological meaning. Third, identify the voice of pain, shifting from one source of authority to another.

Locate

If God resides in our body and dwells within, then we need to learn to live in our bodies as well. All too often, pain drives us out of our bodies. Pain management strategies to deny, divert, and escape our bodies are numerous. The power of "mind over body" is applauded. The message of "no pain, no gain" dominates our thinking. Rarely do we let pain drive us deep into our bodies, deep into the dark interior space where the Unknown and Living God abides. Strangely, those in pain find dark, empty, or black spaces the safest place from which to manage pain. Peter was no exception.

When I asked Peter to locate himself in scripture, to set himself in the context of God's Story, he talked about Job. He pondered for a moment and realized, despite his pain, that Job's God is The Giver of Life and Death, The One Who Gives Breath and The One Who Takes Breath Away. He named Job's God The Faithful One. Peter made another startling discovery. He grasped that the living God held an intimate relationship with him through his pain, just like Job and just like Jesus. He reflected on Jesus and his cross-bearing experience as he moved from pain to beyond Calvary into resurrected joy. Peter said, "Before we started this, I put my pain on the cross. It has been taken off the cross and put at the tomb.

Now, I put it at the tomb, whether inside or out." As he said these words, the still small voice within me rang out, saying, "Whether I fly to the highest heaven or go down to the deepest pit, you are there … for darkness and light are both alike to you" (Psalm 139:1-4). "Blessed be God, El Shammah, The One Who is There!"[18]

Find

If biological words are pregnant with theological meaning, then it is possible to Name God based on these words. For example, Peter described a pain that radiated into his arms. Let us explore the biological word *arms* in scripture to find its theological meaning and discover a Name for God. Three examples follow:

1. "The eternal God is thy refuge, and underneath are the everlasting *arms*: and he shall thrust out the enemy from before thee; and shall say, 'Destroy them'" (Deuteronomy 33:27).

   God is The Refuge. God is Everlasting. God is The Destroyer.

2. "My righteousness is near; my salvation is gone forth, and mine *arm* shall judge the people; the isles shall wait upon me, and on mine *arm* shall they trust" (Isaiah 51:5).

   God is The Righteous One. God is The One Who is Near.
   God is The Savior. God is The Judge. God is The Trustworthy One.

3. "Jesus said to them, 'Suffer the little children to come unto me and forbid them not, for of such is the kingdom of God.' Verily I say unto you, 'Whosoever shall not receive the kingdom of God as a little child, he shall not enter therein.' And he took them up in his *arms*, put his hands upon them, and blessed them" (Mark 10:14-16).

   God is The Sufferer. God is The Compassionate One.
   God is the King. God is The Blesser—Adonai.

All too often we read scripture for good advice rather than Good News. The Good News is that God exists and that God makes His Name know in every generation. In every generation, in every nation, and in every land, we are called to proclaim the Good News. Since the body is the land in which God resides, then we need to proclaim the News of a Living God in that place where pain cries out in distress and agony. When Peter related to his pain as a "monster," his pain intensified. When he connected it with a Name for God, his pain decreased. Through his signal of pain He was able to hear the Good News that God is the Victorious One. Peter realized that his pain gave way to God's "cry of victory."

Identify

If the function of a body part is identified specific to where the pain is felt, then the voice of pain is heard in a relationship with the Living God. Pain is no longer understood from a human point of view, but rather from God's Life arising within us. It shifts from the authority of others to the power of God's Name at work within us. In Peter's case, he heard God's Call for his heart.

Peter learned to convert the function of each part into a Name for God. First, he identified the body part where the pain was felt. Second, he asked himself, "What is the function of the part? What does it do for the body/physical?" And third, he converted the function into a Name for God that he could understand. Sometimes our understanding of God is too small.[19] It is limited by our experience, and we need to open ourselves to God Who is The More.[20] Peter's exploration of his pain through Faith Listening yielded the following discoveries.

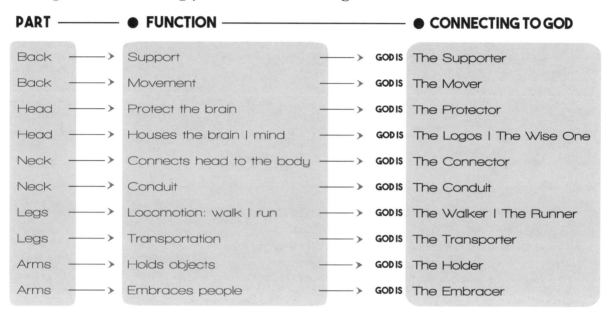

PART	FUNCTION	CONNECTING TO GOD
Back	Support	GOD IS The Supporter
Back	Movement	GOD IS The Mover
Head	Protect the brain	GOD IS The Protector
Head	Houses the brain | mind	GOD IS The Logos | The Wise One
Neck	Connects head to the body	GOD IS The Connector
Neck	Conduit	GOD IS The Conduit
Legs	Locomotion: walk | run	GOD IS The Walker | The Runner
Legs	Transportation	GOD IS The Transporter
Arms	Holds objects	GOD IS The Holder
Arms	Embraces people	GOD IS The Embracer

C | CELEBRATE GOD'S PRESENCE

God's Presence is celebrated when we awaken to God's Life and bless God's Name. Peter started out with an awareness of God Who is One: Father, Son, and Holy Spirit. And yet, he uncovered many Names for God as he experienced the intimacy of God's relationship with him through his pain. Scripture is replete with stories of God's manifestation in physical reality. Moses experienced the Divine Presence of God on Mount Sinai and his face shone (Exodus. 34:2–35). Jesus lived the Divine Presence of God, and it transfigured his body on Mount Tabor. Peter is no exception. He, too, experienced a physical change when he heard "God's Cry for his heart."

Words have power. Theologically, John captures this fact when he states that "In the beginning was the Word, and the Word was with God, and the Word was God" (John 1:1). Scientists confirm biologically that both words and pain trigger neurological responses. A word spoken affects the body/physical. Words activate physiological responses that can reduce or alleviate pain. The words *heavy* and *warm* are used in autogenic training.[21] Hypnosis can produce anesthesia in a body part.[22] Neurolinguistic Programming offers a systematic approach that couples the science of neurology with the study of linguistics to engage the brain for a change.[23] The Faith Factor relies upon using the word *one* or a word associated with God, such as *love*, to elicit the relaxation response and a sense of well-being.[24]

Peter listened to his pain through the power of God's Word and celebrated God's Presence. First, he created a Blessing Litany. Second, he spoke a Breath Prayer. And third, he reflected on God's action in his life through the voice of pain. Peter's Blessing Litany follows:

Peters' Blessing Litany

Blessed are You, Lord God, **The One God.**
Blessed are You, Lord God, **The Giver of Life and Death.**
Blessed are You, Lord God, **Father, Son and Holy Spirit.**
Blessed are You, Lord God, **The Faithful One.**
Blessed are You, Lord God, **The Refuge.**
Blessed are You, Lord God, **The Everlasting One.**
Blessed are You, Lord God, **The Destroyer.**
Blessed are You, Lord God, **The Righteous One.**
Blessed are You, Lord God, **The One Who is Near.**
Blessed are You, Lord God, **The Savior.**
Blessed are You, Lord God, **The Judge.**
Blessed are You, Lord God, **The Trustworthy One.**
Blessed are You, Lord God, **The Sufferer.**
Blessed are You, Lord God, **The Crucified One.**
Blessed are You, Lord God, **The Risen One.**
Blessed are You, Lord God, **The Compassionate One.**
Blessed are You, Lord God, **The King.**
Blessed are You, Lord God, **The Blesser.**
Blessed are You, Lord God, **The Supporter.**
Blessed are You, Lord God, **The Mover.**
Blessed are You, Lord God, **The Protector.**
Blessed are You, Lord God, **The Logos.**
Blessed are You, Lord God, **The Wise One.**
Blessed are You, Lord God, **The Connector.**
Blessed are You, Lord God, **The Conduit.**
Blessed are You, Lord God, **The Walker.**
Blessed are You, Lord God, **The Runner.**
Blessed are You, Lord God, **The Transporter.**
Blessed are You, Lord God, **The Holder.**
Blessed are You, Lord God, **The Embracer.**

Peter's Breath Prayer was, "Blessed are You, Lord God, The Risen One." Peter's reflections culminated in the discovery that his pain was no longer associated with the monster's voice, but rather God's Voice claiming "victory."

Peter placed his pain in the context of God's Life. He became a living text when he realized his pain was not on the cross but rather at the tomb, whether inside or out. The authenticity of Jesus's resurrection became alive. The incarnational reality of the Word made flesh was made manifest. Peter experienced what Paul declared, "You are the epistle of Christ … written not with ink but with the Spirit of the living God; not in tables of stone but in fleshy tables of the heart" (2 Corinthians 3:3).

Hopefully, Peter's example has stimulated your curiosity to apply Faith Listening to your pain or the pain expressed by another person. If so, you are welcome to follow the instructions set out in the Practice Guide 2| Chapter 2| The Body/Physical and the Signal of Pain. As you do so, remember that pain in the body/physical is an indicator of life. So, too, it can be a signal that directs you to God Who is the Life-Giver.

May God, The Incarnate One, be ever present with you!

What is your story of pain? Write it down. Be specific. Describe where it is located in your body/physical. Pay attention to where it starts and where it ends. How do you know you have pain? What is it like? For example, my heart is melting like wax or my stomach is twisted in a knot. You will use this story to discern God's Presence.

_____

_____

_____

_____

A | Awaken to God's Life

There are two ways to awaken to God's Life. The first is sensory awareness and the second is body movement. Let's explore both.

Sensory Awareness

Awaken to the fact that God, The Creator, The Life-Giver, is all around you. Pay attention to your five senses. Let your senses guide you. You may awaken to all five senses or you may be aware of only one or two.

Look   Be aware of what happens in your body/physical when you look at your environment. For example, "I see the blue sky, and I feel my breath deepen."

I see _____ **, and I feel my**_____ .

Listen   Be aware of what happens in your body/physical when you hear a sound. For example, "I hear the sound of water flowing gently downstream, and I feel my stomach relax."

I hear _____ **, and I feel my**_____ .

Touch   Be aware of what happens in your body/physical when you touch something. For example, "I touch a soft pillow, and I feel my eyelids close."

I touch_____ **, and I feel my**_____ .

Taste   Be aware of what happens in your body/physical when you taste your favorite food. For example, "I savor the taste of a peach, and I feel my mouth water."

I taste _____ **, and I feel my**_____ .

Smell   Be aware of what happens in your body/physical when you smell something in nature. For example, "I smell the scent of a flower, and I feel the tension in my shoulders vanish.

I smell _____ **, and I feel my**_____ .

Body Movement

Awaken to the reality that God's Life dwells within you. Sometimes, we feel connected to God's Well-Spring of Life. Other times, we feel disconnected. Discover how the interaction between the two is the dance with God Who is The LORD of The Dance.

Find your Postures

Discover two postures: connect to God and disconnect from God. Let's explore both. Be aware that as the mind goes, so the body/physical follows.

Posture 1: Disconnect

→ Stand as you are able.
→ Think about an experience in which you felt disconnected from God. You may need to remember more than one experience. If so, recall the experiences one at a time.
→ Be aware of your breathing.
→ Be mindful of your posture. Pay attention to the position of your body parts: head, arms, hands, fingers, knees, legs, feet, and toes.
→ Hold this body posture for one breath.
→ Let this disconnection posture go. Shake it off.
→ Breathe deeply three times to clear your mind.

Posture 2: Connect

→ Center yourself.
→ Think about an experience in which you felt connected to God. You may need to remember more than one experience. If so, recall the experiences one at a time.
→ Be aware of your breathing.
→ Be mindful of your posture. Pay attention to the position of your body parts: head, arms, hands, fingers, knees, legs, feet, and toes.
→ Acknowledge this connection posture.
→ Hold this body posture for three deep breaths.
→ Become familiar with this posture. Root yourself in it. Stand on Holy Ground.

Dance with God

Invite God to be your dance partner. Create your sacred dance. Move with God. Let The Living God Who is Ever-Present lead you.

Sacred Dance

→ Adopt Posture 1.
→ Exhale deeply and shake off Posture 1.
→ Move to Posture 2.
→ Explore moving between Posture 1 and 2.
→ When Posture 2 becomes comfortable, hold it for 3 deep breaths.
  You may need a transitional posture. For example, in Posture 1, my hands/arms are clenched at my sides. In Posture 2, my hands/arms are open and raised above my head. In my transitional posture, my hands/arms form in an open circle just below my shoulders. Incorporate this transitional posture into your Sacred Dance. Pay attention to your breath.

Movement Reflection | Ask Yourself

? *What difference does it make when God is your dance partner?*

? *What happens when you embrace God Who is The LORD of The Dance?*

B | Bless God's Name

There are three ways to bless God's Name: locate, find, and identify. Let's explore all three.

① Locate

Set the story of your pain in the context of God's Story. Discover Who God is and How God is actively present with you amidst your pain.

If you could locate your pain story in the Old Testament, where would you place it?

Scripture _____

If you could locate your pain story in the New Testament, where would you place it?

Scripture _____

Read each scripture that you selected. Reflect upon each passage. Ask yourself, "Who is God in this passage?" Name God in each.

Old Testament Scripture _____   **God's Name** _____

New Testament Scripture _____   **God's Name** _____

② Find

Discover biological words pregnant with theological meaning. Start with your pain's signal. Describe where you feel it in your body/physical. If you experience your pain in your back, then back is your biological word. Your pain may radiate to other parts of your body: neck, legs, or arms. Make sure to list all the parts where you experience pain.

Biological Words   _____

_____

_____

Recognize the function of each part. For example, the neck connects the head to the body. The biological word is neck, and its function is to connect. It connects the head to the body.

Biological Word   **Function**

_____   _____

_____   _____

_____   _____

Translate the biological word and its function into God's Name. For example, the biological word is back. It's function is to support. God is The Supporter. God is The Backer. God is The Advocate. Freely associate or use a thesaurus to generate additional names based on the function.

Biological Word	Function	God is... [Theological Meaning]
_____	_____	_____
_____	_____	_____
_____	_____	_____

③ **Identify**

Wonder if your pain has a voice. Be curious. Explore how your pain may be God's communication with you. Just as physical pain calls for the flow of healing resources into the area where pain is located, so too pain may speak of a deeper message for reconciliation and healing. Obviously, **it is important to have pain assessed by a physician to be sure there is no structural or functional damage.**

Communication Reflection | Ask Yourself

?   *What if pain were a signal for God's Life springing up from deep within?*

?   *What if the living God had no voice, or expression, except through the pain signal in your body/physical?*

Listen to your pain. Befriend your pain. First, show gratitude. Thank the pain for its signal. Second, ask that part of you generating the signal, "Are you willing to speak to me?" If yes, ask it to decrease its intensity so you can hear its "still small" voice. If it decreases, it is willing to speak. If it increases, it is not willing to talk at this time. Ask it again later. Third, if it is willing to speak, let it talk to you. It may be silent at first. If so, be patient. Pain is like an infant who has no words. Create a safe space. The signal of pain will find words to voice its message.

Voice of Pain | Ask Yourself

?   *If my pain could speak, what would it say?*

?   *If God spoke through my pain, what would I hear?*

Give voice to each pain signal. Perhaps you described your pain specific to only one area of your body/physical. Perhaps you traced your pain to more than one body part. Let each body part speak for itself.

Biological Word/ Function	Pain's Voice
_____	_____
	_____
_____	_____
	_____
_____	_____
	_____

C | Celebrate God's Presence

There are three ways to come into God's Presence. All draw on the ancient spiritual practice of blessing God. First, create your Blessing Litany. Second, read your Blessing Litany. Third, establish your Blessing Prayer which is a prayer of adoration.

1 Create a Blessing Litany

Transfer the Names of God you discovered in B | Bless God's Name. Each one is a Blessing Statement in your Blessing Litany. Check to be sure there are no pronouns: I, me, mine, ours, or yours at the end of each Blessing Statement. A Blessing Litany is all about God.

Blessing Litany

Blessed are You, LORD God, The_____

Blessed are You, LORD God, The_____

Blessed are You, LORD God, The_____

Blessed are You, LORD God, The One Who_____

Blessed are You, LORD God, The One Who_____

Blessed are You, LORD God, The One Who_____

2 Read your Blessing Litany

Say your Blessing Litany aloud. Inhale to "Blessed are You, LORD God," and exhale to "God's Name" for each Blessing Statement.

Repeat your Blessing Litany silently. Let your rhythmical breath guide you into celebrating God's Presence.

3 Establish your Blessing Prayer

Choose one Blessing Statement from the Blessing Litany that captures your attention or imagination.

Select one that deepens your breath or relaxes your muscles. It may be one that you like best or makes the most sense to you. Open yourself to the reality that God's Spirit, Pneuma, is in every breath you take. Remember: God is Life. Life is Breath. Breath is God.

Blessing Prayer

_____

Breathe your Blessing Prayer, a Prayer of Adoration, through your body. Repeat this prayer three times. Inhale when you say, "Blessed are You, LORD God," and exhale to "God's Name."

Reflect on Your Story

? What difference does it make when you apply Faith Listening to the Body/Physical and your Signal of Pain?

? What happens when you locate your story of pain in the context of God's Life?

? What did you discover when you found biological words pregnant with theological meaning?

? What new insights did you gain when you awaken to God's Life, bless God's Name and celebrate God's Presence?

Other Faith Listening Opportunities

☐ Create a Blessing Litany and a Blessing Prayer based on body parts and functions.
→ Take a piece of paper and make three columns.
→ Column 1: Brainstorm body parts.
→ Column 2: List the function for each body part.
→ Column 3: Convert the body part and the function into a Name for God.
For example, the body part is heart. The function is to pump blood. God's Name is The Sacred Heart, The Pumper, and The Blood Giver.

☐ Invite a friend or family member who experiences pain to let you practice the ABCs of Faith Listening with him/her.

CHAPTER 3 | The Body/Mental and the Capacity of the Mind

....

Let this mind be in you, which was also in Jesus Christ.
—Philippians 2:5

What is the body/mental except a storehouse of knowledge? Knowledge is stored in two ways: a memory bank and a data bank. First, a memory bank of sensory images, sounds, feelings, smells, and tastes are cued by words. These words trigger a biochemical reaction in the brain sending signals to the body/physical. This is known as a mind/body feedback loop. For example, link the words *stove*, *hot*, and *burn* together. Now pay attention to what happens when you say each one separately. Stove: What kind of stove comes to mind? Hot: What physical action is triggered when you hear the stove is hot? Burn: What if you touch the stove anyway and experience the burn?

Second, a data bank of personal experiences and authoritative information work together to provide meaning. This meaning is built upon the teachings of others and the wisdom of the Spirit. Sometimes, this creates conflict. Other times, it provides clarity. In either case, thoughts draw upon the dynamic relationship between head and heart knowledge. That is, head knowledge consists of information gained from disciplined study and authoritative research. Empirical data or factual proof directs the logic. Heart knowledge consists of information gained by living and listening to the still small voice within. Intuition and instinct guide the thinking.

What is the capacity of the mind except an active imagination? Imagination combines both rational and nonrational thought. It draws upon head and heart knowledge when making decisions. Imagination can be our best friend or our worst enemy. The mind can imagine the worst-case and the best-case scenarios. It can plan and set goals. It can judge and perceive. It takes advantage of both conscious and unconscious thought. The mind is proficient at forming opinions and beliefs.

Imagine a belief like the one Paul states: "We have the mind of Christ" (1 Corinthians 2:16). What does this mean? Perhaps it means that we no longer see things from a human point of view but rather from the shared mind-set of Christ. This implies a single focus on God and an openness to the wisdom of God's Spirit. God's Spirit can only disclose the depth of God's Nature. Paul speaks of this reality when he says: "We have received, not the spirit of the world, but the spirit which is of God that we might know the things that are freely given to us of God" (1 Corinthians 2:6–16). This intimate interweaving of God's Life with ours is the norm. This is what the mind's eye needs to see when you go into your memory bank or walk into your informational data bank.

Paul reiterates this theme when he says: "Let this mind be in you that was in Christ Jesus" (Philippians 2:5). Imagine what this could mean. Paul is addressing the collective you to the church in Philippi where there is division and conflict between members. He wanted the people to be of one Body, one Mind, and one Spirit through worship. Paul knows that as we tune our minds to Christ Jesus in unity together, we have a single focus, a single norm, just like the mind that was in Christ Jesus. That is, being one with God, whom Jesus named The Father. Here, we experience harmony before God and humility before others.[25]

Harmony and humility are two capacities of the mind that was in Christ Jesus. Harmony implies that we are in one accord with God, within ourselves, with others, and with creation. It calls for unity and offers a peace that passes all understanding. Humility suggests that a person does not think of him/herself better or worse off than another. It counts all people equal and respects the dignity of all persons. It judges not, but perceives the whole person. Jesus discerned God's Presence, steering his thoughts and actions through a unified relationship with God Who is The Father. He embraced the humanity of each person with compassion.

Compassion is the third capacity of the mind that was in Christ Jesus. This mind operates from the compassionate principles of God's unconditional love, mercy, and hope. It perceives wholeness where there is brokenness. It operates with kindness in times of suffering and comfort in times of sorrow. Jesus remembered God in circumstances of trouble or distress. He was reminded of compassion in times of chaos and confusion whether he wanted to or not.[26] When you find yourself in similar situations, have the mind of Christ. As Paul states, "Be not conformed to this world, but be transformed by the renewing of your mind" (Romans 2:12). Renew your mind by awakening to God's Life, blessing God's Name, and celebrating God's Presence.

A | AWAKEN TO GOD'S LIFE

Renew your mind by awakening to God's Life. Jesus's mind-set or worldview consisted of the reality that life began and ended with God. Nothing—no life—could exist without God. God is The Alpha and The Omega.[27] The mind that was in Christ Jesus had the capacity to see through an experience and to recognize Who God is and What God is doing. It understood that the being of God is equivalent to the doing of God in all circumstances. Can you imagine that you have the mind of Christ within you? Perhaps one of the easiest ways to activate your imagination is to jump into scripture. Let us take a leap of faith and awaken to God's Life. Read Psalm 23 aloud.

¹ The LORD is my shepherd. I shall not want.

² He makes me lie down in green pastures; he leads me beside still waters;

³ He restores my soul. He leads me in right paths for his name's sake.

⁴ Even though I walk through the darkest valley, I fear no evil; for you are with me; your rod and your staff they comfort me.

⁵ You prepare a table before me in the presence of my enemies; you anoint my head with oil; my cup overflows.

⁶ Surely goodness and mercy shall follow me all the days of my life, and I shall dwell in the house of the LORD my whole life long (Psalm 23).

What do you experience from reading Psalm 23? Are you left with a memory of your own similar life experience? Do you feel better once you read the psalm? Is your focus on yourself or upon God?

REFLECTION NOTES —————————— ●

_____

_____

_____

_____

_____

_____

_____

_____

All too often, we read scripture or listen to stories with an acute awareness of our own experiences and our own feelings, rather than tuning into Who God is and What God is doing. Most of us associate our lives with the life of the psalmist rather than with the Life of God. Yet, the psalmist knows no life exists without God. The psalmist points to the Nature of God acting in human experience. So, read Psalm 23 again and awaken to God's Life. Let your mind's eye and ear open to the untold Story of God, working between the lines of the human drama and unfolding in the life of the psalmist. Sometimes, it is obvious. Other times, it requires an ability to listen with ears of faith.

For example, the psalmist states clearly in verse 1 that God is The Shepherd. There is no question Who God is. However, God's identity in verse 4 is not so direct. It reads, "I fear no evil; for you are with me." This passage points to God as _you_ and suggests Who God is by the action _are_. The psalmist awakens us to God Who Is and Was and Evermore Shall Be. Likewise, if our ears hear the word _fear_ and our eyes see the word _evil_, we might read between the lines and conclude that God is The Deliverer or God is The LORD of Hosts.

Let us awaken to God's Life through Psalm 23. Remember, God is the subject of our faith and the focus of our mind's eye. Discover Who God is and What God is doing by underlining the verb or action word in each verse the psalmist writes. Make a list of Who God is by writing down the action(s) in each verse.

ACTIONS ────────── ●

¹ God is _____

² God is _____

³ God is _____

⁴ God is _____

⁵ God is _____

⁶ God is _____

Now that you have begun to awaken to God's Life through the familiar verses of Psalm 23, you may want to know what other people have discovered after awakening to God's Life through Faith Listening. Some have said, "It gives me a sense of peace and comfort." Other readers have said, "It calms me … slows me down." "It provides a sense of safety … a sense of quiet."

Here are some examples with explanations from specific verses in Psalm 23. These will help you fine tune your Faith Listening skill.

¹ *God is The LORD … The Shepherd … The Provider … The Caregiver*

This person uses the text. She accepts the direct statement of the psalmist and identifies God as LORD and Shepherd. Then, she welcomes an indirect approach by thinking about what a shepherd does: provides and cares. The shepherd's role suggests to her a provider and a caregiver.

² *God is The Rest Giver … The Creator*

This person uses free associations to discover Who God is. The phrase *makes me lie down* implies The Rest Giver. The words *green pastures* indicate God is The Creator. Free association can be enhanced with the use of a good thesaurus or a brainstorming session with a good friend.

³ *God is The Strength … The Guide … The Director … The Righteous One.*

This person rephrases the words of this verse after hearing it. She says, "He gives me the strength to follow his direction in a righteous way." It is common to identify with a biblical character and ask, "What is in it for me." This listening technique is called empathy or sympathy. It is a listening skill that requires us to access our own experience to understand the other person. Not so common is to identify with the Life of God working through and in the lives of people, including biblical characters. This listening ability is called Compassionate Listening.[28] It is centered in God's Life and Passion as God responds to human suffering and need. Setting a person's life in the context of God's Life requires an identification with God. Although the first response may be toward the human story, it is possible to employ a feedback listening technique to awaken to God's Life. In this case, the words from the woman's statement: "strength, follow, direction, and righteous" are feedback for her to reflect God's Life. She realized that the psalmist's words were not so much about her as they were about God. She could easily identify that God is The Strength, The Guide, The Director, and The Righteous One.

⁴ *God is The Present One … The Safe One … The Comforting One … The Companion … The Protector.*

This person took seriously the faith assumption that we are formed in the image of God (Genesis 1:27) and the breath of the Almighty gives life (Job 33:4-6). We are because God is, or I am because God is The Great I AM. He completed the statements, "I fear no evil because God You are the Present One; I walk through the darkest valley because God You are Safety." Faith reasoning continued to enlighten his awakening to God's Life when he made the statements: "If l walk through a dark valley, then you are The Companion. If I fear, then you are The Protector."

⁵ *God is The Preparer … The Anointer.*

This person focuses on two actions in the verse: prepare and anoint. At first, she was excited at how easy it was to awaken to the Life of God. Then, she paused and said, "I am not too sure about The Anointer." She indicated that her objection came from an image of an oily head. This objection can be both an obstacle and an opportunity. As an obstacle, it could keep her from awakening to God as Anointer. As an opportunity, it could lead her to embrace this Life of God by finding how she understands anointing. She discovered that for her, oil and anointing were part of the healing ritual through the power of the Spirit. Once she recognized that God is Spirit, she discovered the added life-giving aspect of God Who is The Anointer.

⁶ *God is Good … Merciful.*

This person uses his knowledge of scripture to inform his statement that God is good and merciful. He is familiar with the passage, "For the LORD is good; God's mercy endures forever" (Psalm 100:5a, b). This listening skill to index words used in the Hebrew and Christian Bible depends upon memory. We each have access to an internal concordance based upon our knowledge of scripture. But, it may be a good idea to have one on hand. A Concordance[29] is a resource book for when our memory fails or when our knowledge is limited.

These six responses provide guidance into how to awaken to God's Life. The key is to start with what you know; build on what you have, and set your life in the context of God's Life. Human life and God's Life are two sides of the same coin. On one side, a human tale is told; on the other side, God's Story is heard. Faith Listening is like flipping a coin. Both sides stay together when the coin is tossed. But, when it lands, one side is seen, and the other is unseen. All too often, it is God's Life that remains hidden or unseen when the human tale is being told.

Faith Listening directs your attention to the unseen side of God's Presence while a human tale is being told. The following six guidelines are reminders of how to awaken to God's Life by applying Faith Listening when you read scripture or listen to a story.

6 GUIDELINES ——————— ●

1 Read or listen to a text.
2 Make free associations.
3 Establish an identification.
4 Employ Faith Reasoning.
5 Embrace your objections.
6 Use a resource book.

B | BLESS GOD'S NAME

Blessing God's Name is a matter of plugging in an identified Name of God into the blessing formula. Psalm 23 demonstrates how Blessing Litanies can be formed. A Blessing Litany that follows the six guidelines reads:

Psalm 23 Blessing Litany

1 Blessed are You, LORD God, **The Shepherd.**
Blessed are You, LORD God, **The Provider.**
Blessed are You, LORD God, **The Caregiver.**
2 Blessed are You, LORD God, **The Rest Giver.**
Blessed are You, LORD God, **The One Who Brings Peace.**
3 Blessed are You, LORD God, **The Creator.**
Blessed are You, LORD God, **The One Who Makes Green Pastures.**
Blessed are You, LORD God, **The Almighty.**
Blessed are You, LORD God, **The One Who Gives Strength.**
4 Blessed are You, LORD God, **The Guide.**
Blessed are You, LORD God, **The One Who Lights the Path.**
Blessed are You, LORD God, **The Director.**
Blessed are You, LORD God, **The Righteous One.**
Blessed are You, LORD God, **The Present One.**
5 Blessed are You, LORD God, **The Safe One.**
Blessed are You, LORD God, **The One Who is Comforting.**
6 Blessed are You, LORD God, **The Companion.**
Blessed are You, LORD God, **The Protector.**
Blessed are You, LORD God, **The Preparer.**
Blessed are You, LORD God, **The Anointer.**
Blessed are You, LORD God, **The Merciful One.**
Blessed are You, LORD God, **The One Who is Good.**

Write down your reflections. Describe your physical sensations and emotional responses. What happens to you when you listen with faith to hear the unseen Story of God's Life at work in the author's story as found in Psalm 23? What difference does it make? What changes occurred? What new insights have you gained?

REFLECTION NOTES ⬤

_____
_____
_____
_____
_____
_____
_____
_____

C | CELEBRATE GOD'S PRESENCE

Now create your own Blessing Litany. Jump into scripture. Select a biblical passage, a psalm, or a story to read. First read your selection. Second, review it as an editor and circle the verbs or actions. Convert the action to a Name for God. Add it to the Blessing Litany form below. Remember, God's Name can be both a title such as Judge and an action such as The One Who Judges. In some cases, God's Name is the opposite of the action. For example, God is The One Who Loves when a person says, "I hate you." Be sure to state God's Name for Who God is and What God is doing without reference to yourself. In other words, double check to be sure there are no personal pronouns in your Blessing Litany: I, me, my, mine, you, or ours.

Blessing Litany based on _____

Blessed are You, LORD God, The _____

Blessed are You, LORD God, The _____

Blessed are You, LORD God, The _____

Blessed are You, LORD God, The One Who _____

Blessed are You, LORD God, The One Who _____

Blessed are You, LORD God, The One Who _____

Let your Blessing Litany move through you. Say the Blessing Litany aloud by using your breath. Inhale to "Blessed are You, LORD God," and exhale to "God's Name" for each of your discoveries. Repeat the Blessing Litany silently, paying attention to your breath. Choose one Blessing Statement that deepens your breath and relaxes your muscles. This is your Blessing Prayer. Repeat this Blessing Prayer three times aloud and three times silently in rhythm to your breath. Open your imagination and know that you have the mind of Christ.

My Blessing Prayer is

_____

Now that you have celebrated God's Presence, what difference does it make? What happens when you read between the lines in scripture to discover who this God is that we worship? What is the breadth and depth of God's relationship with you? Have you found unity with God, within yourself, with others, and with creation? Has your capacity for harmony, humility, or compassion increased? What does it mean to let this mind be in you that was in Christ Jesus?

REFLECTION NOTES ───────●

_____

_____

_____

_____

_____

_____

_____

_____

Just as God is Self-revealed in the living text of scripture from Genesis to Revelation, so too, we can discover Who God is and How God moves with us in our daily lives. Not only do you have the mind of Christ, but you are the epistle of Christ, the text, upon which the Spirit of The Living God is writing His Story upon your heart.[30] Paul's epistles encourage people to worship God in harmony and humility. Certainly, we can do the same. Who is this God you worship? How is God Self-disclosing to you considering your everyday life? Continue to discover how you and others are God's Epistles by following the instructions in Practice Guide 3| Chapter 3| The Body/Mental and the Capacity of the Mind.

May God, The All-Knowing One, give you insight and wisdom!

You are an epistle written by God. God is writing His Story on the tablet of your heart. What is your story? Jot down a story about an experience or relationship. Select one that continues to surface no matter how much you wish it would go away.

_____

_____

_____

_____

_____

_____

_____

_____

A | Awaken to God's Life

There are two ways to awaken to God's Life: be an editor and be curious. Both set the content of your story in the context of God's Story. Just like the stories we read in scripture reveal Who God is and What God is doing, so to your story gives way to God's Name and God's Presence.

Be an editor

Look at your story. Start from the end of your story. Read each line from right to left. Circle the verbs (action words) in each sentence.

Be curious

Find a story or passage in scripture that reminds you of your story. For example, if my story is about feeling overwhelmed, I might associate my story with Jonah's story when he was thrown overboard. Read the story you selected. Read it again. This time backwards from right to left and circle the verbs (action) as you go.

B | Bless God's Name

Convert the action words (verbs) from your story and the scripture story into Names for God. List all the verbs that you found. Let each one be a Name for God. Sometimes a verb is negated by an adverb. For example, "I am not worth anything." Let the verb be God's Name: God is The Great I Am or God is The Worthy One.

Action Word	God's Name
_____	_____
_____	_____
_____	_____
_____	_____
_____	_____

C | Celebrate God's Presence

There are three ways to come into God's Presence. All draw on the ancient spiritual practice of blessing God. First, create your Blessing Litany. Second, read your Blessing Litany. Third, establish your Blessing Prayer which is a prayer of adoration.

1 Create a Blessing Litany

Transfer the Names of God you discovered in B | Bless God's Name. Each one is a Blessing Statement in your Blessing Litany. Check to be sure there are no pronouns: I, me, mine, ours, or yours at the end of each Blessing Statement. A Blessing Litany is all about God.

Blessing Litany

Blessed are You, LORD God, The _____

Blessed are You, LORD God, The _____

Blessed are You, LORD God, The _____

Blessed are You, LORD God, The One Who _____

Blessed are You, LORD God, The One Who _____

Blessed are You, LORD God, The One Who _____

2 Read your Blessing Litany

Say your Blessing Litany aloud. Inhale when you say, "Blessed are You, LORD God," and exhale to "God's Name."

Repeat your Blessing Litany silently. Let your rhythmical breath guide you into celebrating God's Presence.

3 Establish your Blessing Prayer

Choose one Blessing Statement from the Blessing Litany that captures your attention or imagination.

Select one that deepenes your breath or relaxes your muscles. Pick one that you like best or makes the most sense to you. Open yourself to the reality that God's Spirit, Pneuma, is in every breath you take. Remember: God is Life. Life is Breath. Breath is God.

Blessing Prayer

_____

Breathe your Blessing Prayer, a Prayer of Adoration, through your body. Repeat this prayer three times. Inhale when you say, "Blessed are You, LORD God," and exhale to "God's Name."

Reflect on Your Story

? What difference does it make when you allow the Body/Mental and the Capacity of the Mind to embrace God's Active Presence?

? What happens when you identify Who God is, What God is doing, and How God is present in your story?

? What new insight did you gain when you awaken to God's Life, bless God's Name, and celebrate God's Presence?

Other Faith Listening Opportunities

☐ Create a Blessing Litany and a Blessing Prayer based on verbs (action words).
  → Take a piece of paper and make two columns.
  → Column 1: Brainstorm a list of action words.
  → Column 2: Convert each action word into a Name for God.
  For example, the action word is *create*. God's Name is The Creator or The One Who Creates.

☐ Listen to a friend's complaint. Invite your friend to work through the ABCs of Faith Listening with you.

☐ Read a scripture passage or a newspaper article. Be an editor and practice Faith Listening to discern God's Presence.

CHAPTER 4 | The Body/Emotional and the Purpose of the Emotions

. . . .

And we know that all things work together for good to them that love God,
to them who are the called according to His purpose.

—Romans 8:28

What is the body/emotional except a connection between physical signals and mental thoughts? An emotion is a glandular response to either an external or internal stimulus that directly triggers an instinctual adaptive response. This response is known as an action or behavior. An external stimulus might be a phone ringing or a flash of lightning. An internal stimulus might be the words you say to yourself or a picture in your mind's eye. Whatever the stimulus, an emotion is e + motion or energy in action.

In other words, an emotion is a visceral or physical reaction to the world around us or to the world within us. An emotion is an internal state of being. The body/physical receives neurological signals from the brain which are designed to energize the body for action. At the same time, these signals are sent to the mind where an emotion is labeled. Once an emotion is labeled, thoughts are triggered and actions follow. Thoughts take the form of images, sounds, sensations, smells, and tastes. Actions are conscious and unconscious. However, when the emotion is experienced, it has a purpose designed to deal with the external or internal stimulus.

What is a purpose except an outcome to be achieved? Originally, emotions were designed for survival purposes. Their goal is to deal with the external stimulus that triggered the emotion. Imagine that the external stimulus is a tiger attacking you. Anger arises instinctually. Its purpose is to destroy. The basic reaction is to fight or flee. Anger provides the necessary energy to destroy the tiger or run before the tiger destroys you. Once action is taken, anger's energy is released. Hormonal balance is restored. The brain and the mind work together to reinstate harmony once an emotion's purpose has been fulfilled.

An emotion's purpose remains the same for either an external or internal stimulus. However, the consequences are different. If the stimulus is external, the purpose is directed outward. If the stimulus is internal, the purpose is directed inward. For example, a friend or a colleague attacks you verbally. You are stunned and caught off-guard. The person turns and walks away. You do your best to return to what you were doing before the attack. However, you replay the scene repeatedly in the merry-go-round of your mind. Now, the stimulus is internal. You can feel your heartbeat increasing, blood pressure rising, and muscles tightening for action. Anger floods through your body/physical and your body/mental imagines the perfect comeback. But, the person is gone, and you are left holding the bag. The anger turns inward. The result is an internal state of dis-ease. Anger's destructive purpose affects you physically, mentally, behaviorally, and spiritually.

Emotions are paradoxical. That is, two opposite things can exist at the same time. Where there is a destructive purpose, there is also a creative purpose. Anger energizes both destructive actions and creative actions. A destructive action would be to scream at someone or throw an object. A creative action would be to play an instrument or paint a picture. Emotions are a natural human response to the world around us and to the world within us. They are neither positive nor negative. Emotions are neither good nor bad. They serve a purpose. Emotions are real. They are a fact of life. They are simply an internal state charged with energy designed for action.

Emotions can be a powerful indicator of God's Life. We know that God is The Creator and Destroyer. If we allow the purpose of an emotion to point us toward God, then emotions link us to God's Purpose for life. By listening to an emotion through the ears of faith, an emotion can awaken us to God's Life, encourage us to bless God's Name, and inspire us to celebrate God's Presence.

A | AWAKEN TO GOD'S LIFE

How does an emotion awaken us to God's Life? There are three basic ways this can occur. First, since an emotion is a physical response to internal and external stimulus, awakening is a matter of awareness. Where is the emotion felt in the body/physical? Second, since an emotion involves thought, awakening is a matter of tuning in to associated words. What story is told about the emotion in the body/mental? Third, since an emotion has a purpose, awakening is a matter of identifying its purpose. What is its purpose, and how does it lead to the directive: Be reconciled to God? (2 Corinthians 5:20).

Since the end target of Faith Listening is to "be reconciled to God," how can an emotion be a doorway to reconciliation? The fact that an emotion travels through a neurological pathway gives us our first key. When an emotion is felt, it has a physical sensation.[31] This sensation has a particular location in the body/physical. The part where the emotion is located has a function it plays on behalf of the whole. This function awakens us to God's Life and points the way to God's Name. Once God's Name is discovered, God's Presence is celebrated and reconciliation to God is complete.

Hannah, age twenty-four, wanted to experience more joy. She reported that over the past five years, she had experienced the death of two family members and one close friend. Often, she would find herself in deep sorrow and grief over her losses. She said that her vision was cloudy and dark. "My eyelids are heavy, and there is no light in my eyes." I asked her to remember a time when she felt joyful. I asked her to think of two more experiences of joy. When I asked her where she experienced joy in her body, she said "through the light in my eyes." I confirmed this because, as she remembered joy, I saw a twinkle in her eyes. As we continued to talk, we reflected on God's Name. Hannah said, "God is Light. God is The Enlightened One." She proceeded to bless God and discovered that God is The Joyful One as well as The Sorrowful One. Hannah identified that it was time to embrace The Joyful One. With this discovery, she entered God's Presence and celebrated a new and joyful life with God.

The fact that an emotion is accompanied by thoughts provides our second key for opening the doorway to reconciliation. When an emotion is felt, it triggers thoughts. These thoughts have a visual picture and an auditory dialogue in the body/mental.[32] Sometimes, smells and tastes are associated with these thoughts. Often, an emotion is labeled and consciously judged good or bad. For example, an emotion is labeled anger. The internal dialogue is "I am angry!" But, what if the words "I am" awaken me to God Who is The Great I AM? What if *angry* awakens me to God Who is The Angry One? The internal dialogue shifts from a human point of view to God's Name. "I am angry, but 'Blessed be You, LORD God, The Angry One." A thoughtful reflection of an emotion through a Breath Prayer allows God's Presence to be celebrated. It causes a different emotion, such as calm, to arise as reconciliation takes place.

Betty, a woman, age twenty-eight, was divorced. She experienced a dream and an emotion that shocked her. The dream was one of skinning her ex-husband alive. She was out for revenge at the way he had replaced her with another woman. This retaliation dream pointed her to the fact that deep down she wanted vengeance. Her thoughts and words awakened her to the fact that "Vengeance is mine says the LORD" (Romans 12:19). She turned this into a Breath Prayer by stating, "Blessed are You, LORD God, The Vengeful One." She became reconciled to the fact that God is not only a Loving God, but a Vengeful God as well. She learned to live in the paradoxical tension between the God of the Old Testament and the God of the New Testament. Relieved of the emotional purpose of vengeance, which is retaliation and punishment, she was set free to live once again with God in love, letting God be The Merciful Judge to take vengeance according to His purpose.[33]

The fact that an emotion is energy in action with a purpose offers our third key for unlocking the doorway to reconciliation. Plutchik's Structural Model of Emotions[34] describes eight basic emotions, each with a specific purpose. All are designed to deal with either external or internal stimulus. The emotions are joy, accept, surprise, fear, sorrow, disgust, expect, and anger. The following chart shows each emotion and its particular purpose.

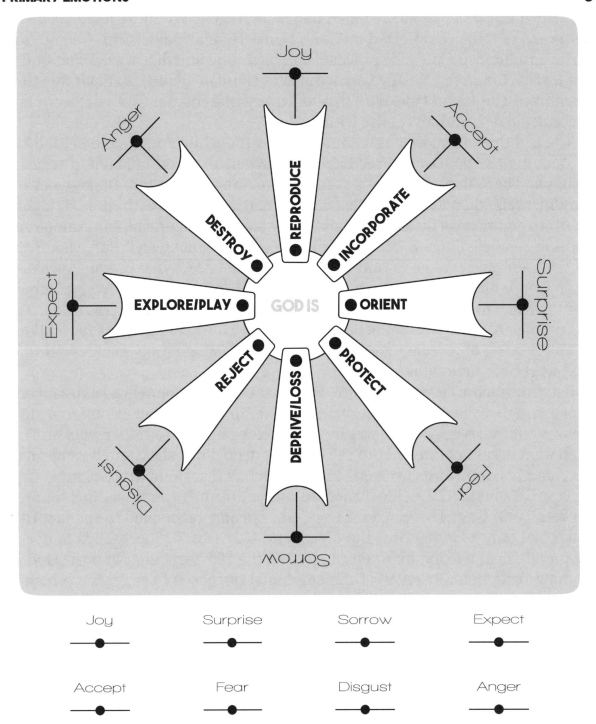

Emotions give color to our lives. An artist purposefully uses harmonious and contrasting colors to enliven his or her artwork. Just so, emotions deal purposefully with internal and external stimulus to create harmonious and contrasting relationships to enrich life. Like the artist's color pallet, these relationships are based on similarities and differences. Similarities tend to create harmony while differences tend to create contrast. Some people find it easier to live in harmony, but others thrive on contrast. As such, some people find it easier to experience the full spectrum of emotions while others shy away or deny certain emotions.

Emotions are a paradox. A paradox is when two oppositional forces are in tension with each other. Both exist at the same time. All too often, when it comes to emotions, one is hidden from view while the other takes center stage. Contrasting emotions make life stimulating, just like contrasting colors give interest to a painting. The key is not to value an emotion as good or bad, but rather to recognize the contrasting emotions and realize their purposes.

Consider the contrasting emotions of joy and sorrow. Their purposes are to reproduce and to deprive, respectively. One woman was in deep sorrow deprived of her husband's company due to his death. This is Henrietta's story. Henrietta, age sixty, was married to Frank for forty-two years. They had been high school sweethearts. Frank died unexpectedly, and, with him, all their retirement plans. This was a double loss. Although she worked and her grandchildren kept her busy, it did not make up for the incredible loneliness she experienced living alone. Henrietta was unable to experience the joy she felt while living with her husband and best friend. Just when she remembered their joy in each other, it dissolved into sadness as quickly as it appeared. Although her sisters in faith were a great support, she doubted she would ever feel joy again.

Henrietta was aware that something needed to be different. Her connection to life was slipping away. It was associated symbolically with Frank. As Henrietta learned to awaken to God's Life moving through her relationship with Frank, joy returned. For each significant event in their lives, she blessed God. Her marriage vow to be husband and wife reminded her that God is The Husband. The birth of her children recalled the fact that God is The Creator. Frank's faithfulness over the years evoked the reality that God is The Faithful One and that God is the Ever-Present One. God became her source of strength, The Strong One, and comfort, The Comforter. When she looked at pictures and memories arose, it was not that her sorrow stopped, but rather she was free to experience the contrasting emotion of joy. Henrietta found, as the psalmist sings:

> [11] Thou hast turned for me my mourning into dancing: thou hast put off my sackcloth, and girded me with gladness;

> [12] To the end that [my] glory may sing praise to thee, and not be silent. O LORD my God, I will give thanks to (and bless) thee forever (Psalm 30).

HENRIETA'S STORY contrasting emotions ⎯⎯⎯⎯⎯⎯⎯⎯⎯⎯⎯⎯⎯⎯ ●

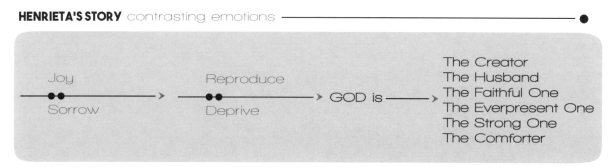

Emotions are complex. One emotion can be a blend of two different emotions with two specific purposes. These are called **paired emotions**. It is like the color purple. Purple is a blend of red and blue. When you mix colors, you get another color. Likewise, when you mix emotions, you get a different emotion. For example, awe is a mixture of surprise and fear whose purpose is to orient and to protect, respectively. In other words, often when awe is no longer felt, other emotions will surface. The results can cause mental confusion and conflicting emotions. Refocusing on the purpose of an emotion, provides an avenue to practice the ABCs of Faith Listening.

Consider the emotion of awe. A woman was experiencing an emotional roller-coaster ride after her experience living through a forest fire. This is her story. Janet, age forty-eight, lived in a beautiful home on top of a plateau overlooking a deep, rocky canyon. At the bottom of the canyon was a river. On the other side of the canyon, a raging forest fire was rapidly approaching. She had been watching its progress for four days, and the fire service was calling for an evacuation of her property. On the surface, it was difficult to believe that the fire would jump the canyon, but the winds were strong. She wondered what to do—stay or leave? The threat was real, instilling fear in Janet. She was terrified at the prospect of losing her home. But, as she watched the fire drawing near, she was filled with a sense of awe at the way the flames jumped from tree to tree, exploding like fireworks in the night. Janet learned that fear is not simply fear. She discovered that there is a fine line between fear that terrorizes and immobilizes and awe that inspires and surprises. One freezes. The other frees.

When the firefighters arrived on the scene, she was surprised. They were unexpected. Two news reporters knocked on the door and asked if they could have a birds-eye view of the fire. She invited them in. With her emotion of fear swirling from awe to terror to surprise, Janet found comfort in the reality that the firemen were there to protect, and the news reporters were there to report the facts. Suddenly, without warning, the winds shifted and brought pouring rain. Relief from the tension of the emotional ups and downs came with the rains. The decision to stay was an easy one, thanks to the elements of nature and the service of people around her. In processing her emotions, Janet reflected on how they were powerful indicators of God's Presence. She discovered that God is The Consuming Fire, The Protector, The Orienteer, and The Creator.

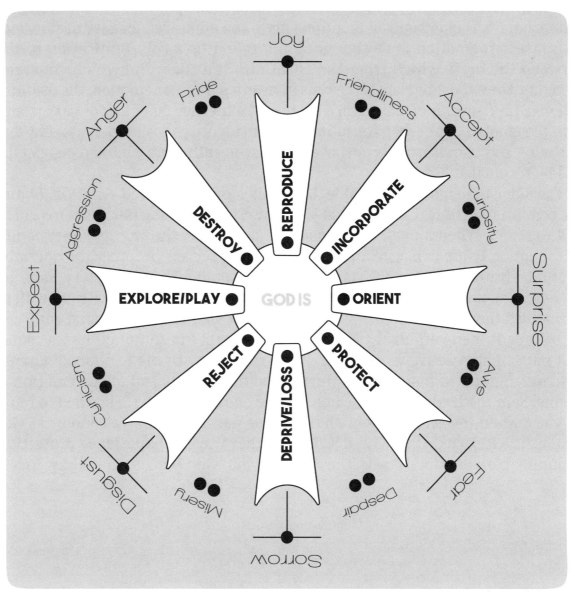

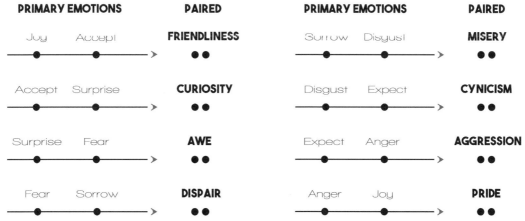

PRIMARY EMOTIONS		PAIRED	PRIMARY EMOTIONS		PAIRED
Joy	Accept	**FRIENDLINESS** ●●	Sorrow	Disgust	**MISERY** ●●
Accept	Surprise	**CURIOSITY** ●●	Disgust	Expect	**CYNICISM** ●●
Surprise	Fear	**AWE** ●●	Expect	Anger	**AGGRESSION** ●●
Fear	Sorrow	**DISPAIR** ●●	Anger	Joy	**PRIDE** ●●

Emotions are an internal state. An internal state is simply a physiological sensation with mental images and sounds. Its boundary is your skin. Its territory is internal. Its flag is neutral. Emotions are to be embraced as a natural human response. An emotion is neither good nor bad. It is a communication bridge between the brain which triggers sensations and the mind which generates thoughts. Once the mind labels the sensation as a particular emotion, the resulting action is predetermined based on a catalog of experienced behaviors associated with the emotion. But, when the mind learns to identify the emotion as a physical sensation and searches for its purpose, it is easy to shift from a human perspective and be reconciled to God.

Consider the emotion of shame. Shame is a **once removed emotion**. Shame is a combination of fear and disgust with the corresponding purposes to protect and to reject. When a person is consumed by shame, the energy generated by this emotion tends to isolate and divide. Keeping secrets becomes the operative relational framework. A man was consumed by shame. This is his story. Sam, age fifty-six, was raised on shame and fed a steady diet of it while growing up with an alcoholic father. He had internalized the voice of shame instilled at an early age. He self-medicated with drugs and alcohol to shut it up. Although he was sober and participated actively in AA, he still struggled with his feelings of shame. Discovering how to focus on the purpose of disgust instead of the emotion of shame, Sam realized that he was not the one being rejected. He learned to reject its voice when the sensations of shame arose and to use his voice to bless God Who is The Rejected One. Sam developed other ways to experience protection, including blessing God Who is The Protector and God Who is The Safety Zone.

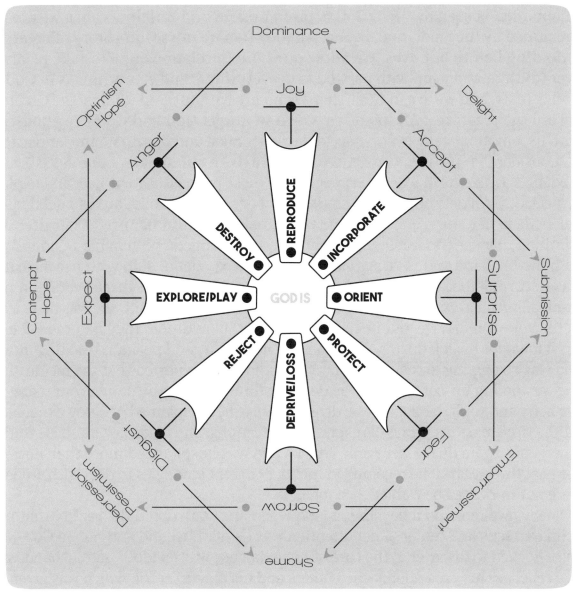

PRIMARY EMOTIONS	ONCE REMOVED	PRIMARY EMOTIONS	ONCE REMOVED
Joy — Surprise	**DELIGHT** ●●	Sorrow — Expect	**DEPRESSION/PESSIMISM** ●●
Accept — Fear	**SUBMISSION** ●●	Disgust — Anger	**CONTEMPT/HOPE** ●●
Surprise — Sorrow	**EMBARRASSMENT** ●●	Expect — Joy	**OPTIMISM/HOPE** ●●
Fear — Disgust	**SHAME** ●●	Anger — Accept	**DOMINANCE** ●●

Emotions awaken us to God's Life. Emotions are powerful indicators of God's Presence hidden beneath the surface. They reveal the Mystery of God within us. An emotion is seen and felt. God is often unseen and unfelt because we are so consumed by the emotional drama. All too often we miss God's Story of creation unfolding before our eyes. We allow our human relationships to take priority over God's relationship with us. God is in everything, and everything is in God.[35] God is in us, and we are in God. There is no life without God. God is The Creator. We are the creatures. All too often, when we forget God and God's relationship with us, emotions take over. They get out-of-control and dominate the landscape.

Consider the emotion of anxiety. Anxiety is a **twice removed emotion**. Specifically, anxiety is a mixture of fear and expectation whose purpose is to protect and to play, respectively. Anxiety became the landscape of one woman whose anxiety debilitated her. This is her story. Mary, age sixty-two, painted a dim picture of her life. She admitted that she was not living in a healthy environment, both in her relationship with her husband and in the city of his choice. The relationship with her husband was in turmoil because of his adulterous affair over the past three years and the death of his mistress. Mary still lived with and loved her husband. She was dedicated to the vow of marriage, but he had shut her out. In addition, they had moved to a rural town for his job during this time. She had left a good position teaching music and was struggling to rebuild her music studio. Mary reported that the medication she was taking for her anxiety was doing nothing to keep the panic from rising in her body and soul. Her health was deteriorating. She complained of being exhausted all the time and was prone to respiratory infections. She made several trips to the emergency room due to her panic attacks and was hospitalized more than once in the past three years. She recognized that her current strategies to deal with anxiety were not working. She wanted a change.

Mary awakened to a new life in God when she confronted the reality that her primary focus and center of her attention was on her husband and not on God. She was shocked to discover at the core of her existence was an idol—her husband. She had relied on his protection, which failed, and his playful spirit, which was given to another. She was anxious that she would be left alone, and she expected the worst. By learning to explore her anxiety as an indicator of God's Presence, Mary learned that anxiety was a combination of two primary emotions: fear and expect. She discovered that fear's purpose is to protect, and expect's purpose is to explore. Instead of being paralyzed, she aligned with God Who is The Protector and God Who is The Explorer.

First, Mary became familiar with the signals of fear in her body/physical. She took action to relieve them when she felt the early warning signs. They became reminders to focus on God as the center of her life and to worship God through Breath Prayers, movement, and playing the piano. Second, Mary embraced exploration by using her musical skills to deepen God's relationship with her. She discovered the conflicting voices of others that led to her anxiety through the vibration of the piano.

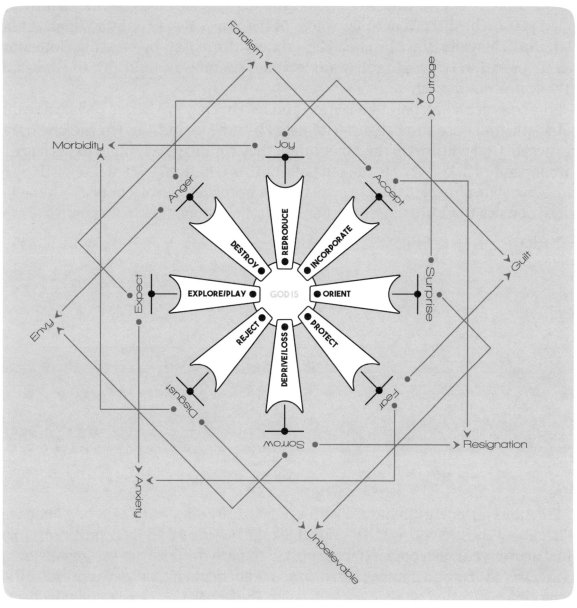

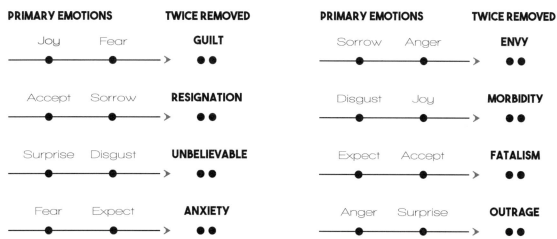

PRIMARY EMOTIONS		TWICE REMOVED		PRIMARY EMOTIONS		TWICE REMOVED
Joy	Fear	**GUILT** ●●		Sorrow	Anger	**ENVY** ●●
Accept	Sorrow	**RESIGNATION** ●●		Disgust	Joy	**MORBIDITY** ●●
Surprise	Disgust	**UNBELIEVABLE** ●●		Expect	Accept	**FATALISM** ●●
Fear	Expect	**ANXIETY** ●●		Anger	Surprise	**OUTRAGE** ●●

She connected with God's resonate voice in the deep rich tones of the bass keys and uncovered her own voice in a melody that sang in harmony. As she improvised on the piano. the discord of other voices in her musical ear could not distract her from God's Movement within her. Her anxiety decreased by blessing God. Mary was surprised to realize that her anxiety had become an indicator of God's Life actively present for her.

Emotions are a link between heaven and earth. They are both a physical reality and a spiritual encounter that participates in the Life of God. On the one hand, they locate God within. On the other hand, they capture the human experience. It is important to ask, "What is the purpose of this emotion?" when integrating the two. You can brainstorm the purpose by free association, select one from the list below, or use a thesaurus to find other words. Select one that makes sense to you.

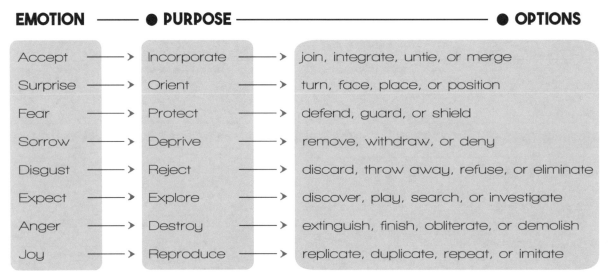

EMOTION	● PURPOSE	● OPTIONS
Accept →	Incorporate →	join, integrate, untie, or merge
Surprise →	Orient →	turn, face, place, or position
Fear →	Protect →	defend, guard, or shield
Sorrow →	Deprive →	remove, withdraw, or deny
Disgust →	Reject →	discard, throw away, refuse, or eliminate
Expect →	Explore →	discover, play, search, or investigate
Anger →	Destroy →	extinguish, finish, obliterate, or demolish
Joy →	Reproduce →	replicate, duplicate, repeat, or imitate

Emotions are energy in motion with a purpose. By now, you might be wondering, "What about those emotions that are not listed? How do I find their purposes?" You will discover your own emotional purposes. You are the one who assigns meaning. You are free to choose a purpose based on your experience rather than those identified in the charts or listed on the previous page. The key is to embrace the purposeful nature of an emotion by awakening to God's Life and blessing God's Name.

B | BLESS GOD'S NAME

There are two ways to bless God's Name. First, the emotion suggests God's Name. If the emotion is love, then God is Love. If the emotion is trust, then God is The Trustworthy One. If the emotion is fear, then God is The Fearful One. Give your emotion to God by blessing God's Name. Second, the emotion's purpose implies God's Name. If the purpose is to protect, then God is The Protector. If the purpose is to reject, then God is The Rejected One. If the purpose is to destroy, then God is The Destroyer and, paradoxically, The Creator. Give your emotion and its purpose to God by blessing God's Name.

Emotions are powerful indicators of God's Presence. Whether you are telling a story or talking about a relationship, emotions are a fact of life. Even scripture is replete with emotions. Not only humans have emotions, but God Self-reveals with an emotional nature such as The Jealous One. First, there is a distinction to be made. It is important to recognize the difference in purpose between a human emotion and the nature of God's Character named with an emotional descriptor. Second, a shift needs to take place between the visceral experience of the emotion and the meaning assigned to the emotion.

First, human jealousy is described as a green-eyed monster. It is a mixture of anger and fear whose purpose is to destroy and protect. The purpose of jealousy is to possess. The human, when jealous, tends to possess through punishment or retaliation. God's jealous nature is tempered by compassion and mercy.[36] It is a direct result of God's immense love described in His covenant relationship with His people. It is not an emotion, but rather a consuming zeal for His people. Jealous is not to be confused with jealousy. The word *jealous*—quanna᷄—is used to describe God's Character in the context of idolatry, which is considered spiritual adultery. God says, "I am the LORD your God ... for I am a Jealous God. Thou shalt have no other Gods before me" (Exodus 20:1–6).

Second, human emotions can dim one's perceptions and cloud one's judgments. Perhaps you were so jealous that you wanted revenge or so angry that you could not think straight. There is a fine line physically as well as spiritually when you shift from being possessed by a human emotion to being passionate about connecting to God. When you acknowledge your anger and bless God, a new emotion arises. For example, consider the fact that God's Name is "I AM that I AM." Acknowledge the emotion by stating, "I am angry, but You, God, are The Angry One!" Continue to focus on God by recalling God's Actions. I remember when you, LORD God, were provoked to anger in the wilderness and in Horeb (Deuteronomy 9:7–8). I remember when you, LORD Jesus, threw the money changers, in righteous anger, out of the temple proclaiming: "My house shall be called the house of prayer; but, you have made it a den of thieves" (Luke 19:45).

Be consumed by God's Life and not by your emotion. Let God be the center of your attention. Let go and let God. Let your focus shift from your emotion to blessing God and celebrating God's Presence. Let us practice finding God's Name by using an emotion, and then make the shift by blessing God's Name. Follow the instructions below to experience how an emotion can point to and participate in God's Life within you.

Go directly by using the name of the emotion. My emotion is joy. I am joyful, but you, God, are The Joyful One. God is The Joyful One. Blessed are You, LORD God, The Joyful One.

DIRECT ——————— ● name

My emotion is _____

I am _____, but You, God, are _____

God is _____

Blessed are You, LORD God, _____

Go indirectly by identifying the purpose of the emotion. My emotion is joy. Its purpose is to reproduce or to re-create. God is The Reproducer. God is The Creator. Blessed are You, LORD God, The Creator.

INDIRECT ——————— ● purpose

My emotion is _____

It's purpose is to _____

God is _____

Blessed are You, LORD God, _____

There are three additional ways to discover how your emotions connect you to God.

1. Go physically by describing the sensations of the emotion. My emotion is joy. The physical sensation is that my eyes open to let in more light. God is the All-Seeing One. God is Light. Blessed are You, LORD God, The Wise One. Blessed are You, LORD God, The Giver of Light.

PHYSICAL ——————— ● sensations

My emotion is _____

The physical sensation is _____

God is _____

Blessed are You, LORD God, _____

2. Go mentally by telling your story about the emotion, including your thoughts. My emotion is joy. My story is about giving birth to my first child. I remember when he was placed upon my stomach to cut the umbilical cord. I felt such immense joy and happiness. I thought, "Wow! This is incredible. This is what life is all about. I am satisfied." God is The Incredible One. God is Life. God is The Satisfier. Blessed are You, LORD God, The Awesome One.

MENTAL ———— ● your story

My emotion is _____

My story is about _____

My thoughts include _____

God is _____

Blessed are You, LORD God, _____

3. Go scripturally by looking up the emotion. My emotion is fear … anxiety. "The fear of the LORD is the beginning of wisdom and the knowledge of the holy is understanding" (Proverbs 9:10). God is Wisdom. God is All-Knowing. God is Holy. Blessed are You, LORD God, The Wise One. Blessed are You, LORD God, The All-Knowing One. Blessed are You, LORD God, The Holy One.

SCRIPTURAL ———— ● theological

My emotion is _____

My scripture is _____

God is _____

Blessed are You, LORD God, _____

C | CELEBRATE GOD'S PRESENCE

Celebrate God's Presence by creating a Blessing Litany and by using a Breath Prayer. Perhaps, you are familiar with both after reading other chapters. In this chapter, you have already started the beginning of a Blessing Litany by acknowledging one emotion. You are welcome to use the Blessing Statements you discovered in the previous section or brainstorm additional Names for God.

Blessing Litany based on _____

Blessed are You, LORD God, The _____

Blessed are You, LORD God, The _____

Blessed are You, LORD God, The One Who _____

Blessed are You, LORD God, The One Who _____

Say your Blessing Litany aloud. Slowly, inhale to "Blessed are You, LORD God," and exhale to "God's Name" for each Name you discovered. Select one Blessing Statement that resonates deeply within your soul. Find one that lets you breathe deeply and relaxes your muscles.

My Blessing Prayer is

_____

Say your Blessing Prayer aloud three times and three times silently to yourself in rhythm to your breath. Open to God's Live-Giving Spirit through the power of your breath.

Make some notes to yourself about what you experienced. Describe your physical sensations and write down your thoughts. What difference does it make when you consider your emotion in the light of celebrating God's Presence?

REFLECTION NOTES ———————— ●

_____
_____
_____
_____
_____
_____
_____
_____

Congratulations! You have explored how an emotion is e+motion or energy in action. It is an internal state with the purpose of leading you to a Name for God and an experience of God's Presence. If you want to deepen your Faith Listening ability, follow the instructions outlined in the Practice Sheet 4| Chapter 4| The Body/Emotional and the Purpose of Emotions. You are welcome to reflect on another emotion by writing about your experience, or you can choose to reflect on another person's emotion as he/she described it to you. Whichever you choose, bear in mind that the human story is set in the context of God's Story. You are the living text of God's Word, just like in scripture. The key is to shift perspectives, no longer seeing things from a human point of view, but seeing from God's Salvation History (2 Corinthians 5:16–17). Faith Listening discerns on How God is active and present in each person's story.

May God, The Passionate One, rise life within you!

Explore how your emotions lead you to God's Name and into God's Presence. First, write a few statements about an emotional experience or relationship. Select one that troubles you or continues to surface despite your best efforts. Be sure to record your emotional feelings, mental thoughts, and physical sensations. Second, practice Faith Listening by following the ABC guidelines.

_____

_____

_____

_____

_____

_____

_____

_____

A | Awaken to God's Life

There are five ways to awaken to God's Life through an emotion: name, purpose, sensations, thoughts, and scripture. Take a few deep breaths. Attune to How God is actively present through your emotions. Use the charts in Chapter 4 to identify the purpose for each emotion. Remember, some emotions are a combination of two primary emotions. For example, shame is the paring of two primary emotions: fear and disgust. Each emotion has a separate pupose: to protect and to reject, respectively.

1 Name
Go directly by identifying the name of the emotions. Circle the emotions in your story. Choose one.

My emotion is _____

2 Purpose
Go indirectly by identifying the purpose of the emotion. If it is a paired emotion, once removed, or twice removed, write the purpose for each.

The purpose of my emotion is _____

3 Sensations
Go physically by describing the physical sensation(s) of the emotion.

The physical sensation(s) of my emotion is (are) _____

_____

4 Thoughts
Go mentally by recognizing thought(s) triggered by the emotion.

The thought(s) triggered by my emotion is (are) _____

_____

Scripture

Go theologically by looking up your emotion or by finding a parallel story in scripture.

Old Testament_____

New Testament_____

B | Bless God's Name

Let Faith Listening activate your emotions. Take a few deep breaths. Convert your discoveries into God's Name. It is important to remember that God's Nature or Character can be described by an emotional descriptor. For example, a primary emotion is joy. Joy's purpose is to reproduce. God's Name is The Producer.

	Discoveries	God's Name
Emotion	_____	_____
Purpose	_____	_____
Sensation	_____	_____
Thought	_____	_____
Scripture: OT	_____	_____
Scripture: NT	_____	_____

C | Celebrate God's Presence

There are three ways to come into God's Presence. All draw on the ancient spiritual practice of blessing God. First, create your Blessing Litany. Second, read your Blessing Litany. Third, establish your Blessing Prayer which is a prayer of adoration.

Create a Blessing Litany

Transfer the Names of God you discovered in B | Bless God's Name. Each one is a Blessing Statement in your Blessing Litany. Check to be sure there are no pronouns: I, me, mine, ours, or yours at the end of each Blessing Statement. A Blessing Litany is all about God.

Blessing Litany

Blessed are You, LORD God, The _____

Blessed are You, LORD God, The _____

Blessed are You, LORD God, The _____

Blessed are You, LORD God, The One Who _____

Blessed are You, LORD God, The One Who _____

Blessed are You, LORD God, The One Who _____

② **Read your Blessing Litany**

Say your Blessing Litany aloud. Inhale when you say, "Blessed are You, LORD God," and exhale to "God's Name."

Repeat your Blessing Litany silently. Let your rhythmical breath guide you into celebrating God's Presence.

③ **Establish your Blessing Prayer**

Choose one Blessing Statement from the Blessing Litany that captures your attention or imagination.

Select one that deepens your breath or relaxes your muscles. Pick one that you like best or makes the most sense to you. Open yourself to the reality that God's Spirit, Pneuma, is in every breath you take. Remember: God is Life Life is Breath. Breath is God.

Blessing Prayer

_____

Breathe your Blessing Prayer, a Prayer of Adoration, through your body. Repeat this prayer three times. Inhale when you say, "Blessed are You, LORD God," and exhale to "God's Name."

Reflect on Your Story

? What happens when you identify Who God is, What God is doing, and How God is actively present in your emotion?

? What difference does it make to embrace God through your Body/Emotional and the Purpose of Emotions?

? What new insights did you gain when you practiced the ABCs of Faith Listening?

Other Faith Listening Opportunities

☐ Create a Blessing Litany and a Blessing Prayer based on emotions.
   → Take a piece of paper and make three columns.
   → Column 1: Brainstorm a list of emotions.
   → Column 2: Identify the purpose of the emotion.
   → Column 3: Convert each emotion and purpose into a Name for God.
   For example, depression is a combination of sorrow and expect. The purpose of sorrow and expect is loss and play, respectively. God is The One Who Grieves and God is The Playful One. The word depression may suggest God is The One Who Presses On. Also, God's Name can be the opposite of depression: God is Hope.

☐ Listen to a family member talk about his/her emotions. Apply the ABCs as you listen. Invite your family member to join you in creating a Blessing Litany and a Blessing Prayer.

☐ Listen to a radio broadcast or watch a podcast. Tune into a new story. Write down the emotions that you hear or see within the story. Practice the ABCs of Faith Listening.

CHAPTER 5 | The Body/Behavioral and the Intent of Behaviors

Take delight in the LORD and He will give you your heart's desire.
—Psalm 37:4

What is the body/behavioral except a person's expression of the dynamic interaction between his/her emotional energy, mental capacity, physical ability, and spiritual symbols? A behavior is the outward or inward expression of this interaction generated by an emotion which is energy in motion. Behaviors are both simple and complex. A person raises his/her voice, and you react in kind by raising your voice or doing the opposite by going silent. Perhaps a person hears a word and assumes it means one thing, but the storyteller means something else.

A behavior connects us to the world within and around us. It is a tangible way in which we express our humanity. A behavior is an indicator of a living relationship. This relationship may be interpersonal or intrapersonal in nature. It may be one that includes God, others, self and/or creation. A person receives devastating news, and you respond by offering a shoulder to cry upon. Perhaps a person suffers a hurt, and he/she cries uncontrollably alone in the silence.

A behavior is a response to life born out of instinct and intent. Instinctually, the limbic brain triggers behaviors intended for survival purposes. The human brain is wired biologically for life. A stimulus occurs, and we react to a threat without thinking. A person sees a drowning dog and jumps into the icy lake to save the dog. Intentionally, the mind selects behaviors that enhance life. The human mind is wired psychologically to generate options based on an intent. A person cannot find work in one city and decides to move to a new city with the intent of finding a good job.

What is intent except your heart's desire to achieve a specific goal? Sometimes, this intent is conscious. Other times, it is unconscious. Either way, a behavior is linked to a positive intent when it is first expressed. A child runs out into the street in the path of an oncoming car, and the parent screams, "Stop!" The parent's heart's desire is for the child to live. The goal is to stop the child. The intent is to protect. In this situation, the behavior of screaming achieves the desired result—life.

But, what happens if the parent continues to scream at the child when no life-threatening situation exists? Eventually, the child learns to ignore the parent. The behavior loses its effectiveness when the intent is separated from the behavior. It is like someone who cries "wolf." When a parent screams at a child in the grocery store to stop crying, the intent to protect no longer matches the behavior. If a parent realizes that the child's cry is one intended for comfort, he/she will select a behavior that comforts the child and stops the crying.

The original intent determines the behavior no matter the context or the judgment, whether it is good or bad. Harmful behavior such as smoking carries with it an original intent. Whoever liked the taste of cigarettes when the first drag was taken? Rather, most smoking starts with peer pressure to belong or to be cool. Eventually, it leads to nicotine addiction. Breaking habitual behaviors or changing a behavior depends on becoming aware of its original intent.

The original intent of Faith Listening is to discover Who God is and How God is active in present reality. Present reality shows itself in behaviors. Behaviors are an expression of life unfolding before our eyes. God is the source of all life. God's Life is intertwined with the human experience. If we allow a behavior to point us toward God through its intent, then behaviors can be powerful indicators of God's Life. By understanding behaviors through the lens of faith, a behavior can awaken us to God's Life, encourage us to bless God's Name, and inspire us to celebrate God's Presence.

A | AWAKEN TO GOD'S LIFE

How does a behavior awaken us to God's Life? First, specify one behavior. It is important to name one behavior, since behaviors have a domino effect, creating a chain reaction that links one behavior to another. Second, identify the original intent of the behavior. Behaviors contain something good or beneficial for the person when they are first expressed. The context or situation in which the behavior is acted out may call for a behavioral option to match its original intent. And third, recognize the underlying instinctual behavior. Instinctual behaviors are hardwired into all living creatures for survival or life-giving purposes.

1. **Specify one behavior.**

    Let us examine the instinctual behavior of sucking and how, for one person, it leads to the learned behavior of nail biting. Sucking is a survival strategy that is hardwired from birth. The baby sucks on the mother's breast, which produces milk with the intent to sustain life. The behavioral action of sucking not only nourishes the baby, but it also protects the child with antibodies. If the urge to suck is not met by the mother presenting her breast, the baby will find another way to satisfy this urge. The baby's mouth and thumb find each other, and the sucking continues. The instinctual behavior, sucking, is the same, but the original intent to sustain life is not.

    Sucking is a life-sustaining, instinctual behavior. It is hardwired in the brain. But, at a certain age, the baby's exploratory behavior of thumb sucking is no longer socially acceptable. As the child grows, learned behaviors are substituted. Sometimes, the behavioral correlation is direct, such as sucking on a straw to drink milk or sucking on a piece of chocolate candy to elevate sugar levels. Other times, it is indirect such as sucking on a cigarette to be part of life with the gang or unconsciously biting fingernails to self-identify when others dominate or dictate what to do and how to do it. In these cases, the instinctual behavior, sucking, is no longer connected to its original intent to sustain life.

2. **Identify the original intent.**

Behaviors contain an original intent.[37] The intent may be conscious or unconscious. It may be attached directly or indirectly to the behavior. A behavior, when first expressed, has a beneficial or good intent for the person. A behavior may turn harmful or self-destructive when it is disassociated from its original intent. Sucking on a straw to drink milk is one thing; sucking on a straw to drink an alcoholic beverage is another. Both are beneficial, if you need calcium or relief, respectively; both may be harmful, if you are lactose intolerant or an alcoholic, respectively. If the original intent of sucking is to sustain life, then unlocking the behaviors associated with the original intent may be complex.

Behaviors are complex. One can be linked to another in an unconscious effort to satisfy the original intent. It is like playing on a baseball team. Every player goes to bat, but not every player hits a home run. Likewise, not every behavior remains connected to its original intent. For example, sucking's original intent is to sustain life. First, the infant sucks milk from the mother's breast or a bottle. Bottle substitutes satisfy the sucking behavior's original intent. Second, the baby sucks on her thumbs, fingers, or toes, but the intent is different: self-discovery. Third, a parent gives the child a pacifier to suck on with the intent of keeping the baby quiet. Fourth, the toddler grabs a sippy cup to drink that is filled with milk. Fifth, the preschooler discovers that sucking on her thumb is no longer acceptable and she adopts another behavior learned from her mother: biting her fingernails. Sixth, the teenager wants to fit in and mimics her peers by smoking cigarettes. Seventh, the young adult wants to be the life of the party and drinks alcohol to release her inhibitions. Eighth, her adult-self copes with stress by sucking on too many pieces of dark chocolate. And so it goes over a lifetime. Substitute behaviors are adopted and layered onto each other without benefit of satisfying the original intent of the instinctual behavior.

3. **Recognize the underlying instinctual behavior.**

Complex behaviors such as the examples above are grounded in instinctual behaviors.[38] Instinctual behaviors do not need any thought or consciousness. They are innate to the human being.

Creatures, including the human being, are born with instinctual behaviors. They exist without any experience or training. Instinctual behaviors are hardwired into the species for life-giving purposes.

A kangaroo baby is born and immediately hops into its mother's pouch. A human baby is born and immediately grasps a finger of another person when it is put into the baby's hand. Have you heard the expression "Let go and let God?" This may be more difficult than it sounds because the instinctual behavior of grasping to clutch and to hold on runs contrary to the learned behavior of releasing to let go.

Likewise, the statement "Get a grip!" may point us to what is most life-giving in experiences of chaos and confusion. The underlying message may be, "Hold onto life, for God is Life; God is a God of order not chaos." There is no doubt that in these situations we need to grasp God's finger and hold on for dear life. But, all too often, we cling to the human and seize the finger of our feelings.

The instinctual impulse to not only survive but to thrive runs deep within the cellular structure of the human body. In other words, instinct is hardwired so that we can survive and cope with our environment. Impulses to act trigger primal instinctual behaviors:[39] grasping, sucking, reproducing, competing, nesting, and caring. These are behaviors that emerge without any training or education.

Instinctive behaviors do not need cognition or consciousness. They are inborn patterns characteristic of all species, including the human being. However, when instinctual and learned behaviors become conscious, it is possible to become aware of their intent and awaken to God's Life. It is at this time that God's Name is recognized. When God's Name is reflected in the behavior, it is only natural to turn toward God and bless God's Holy Name. David shows the way when he says, "Bless the LORD, O my soul: And all that is within me, bless his Holy Name" (Psalm 103:1).

B | BLESS GOD'S NAME

How does a behavior reflect a Name for God? First, select a behavior. Second, identify the behavior's original intent. Third, recognize the underlying instinctual behavior. Fourth, discover God's Name revealed in the behavior. And fifth, bless God's Name. An example follows:

Behavior	⟶	hug
Original Intent	⟶	show affection
Instinctual Behavior	⟶	caring
God's Name	⟶	The Caregiver, The Affectionate One, The Embracer
Blessing Litany	⟶	Blessed are You, LORD God, **The Caregiver.**
		Blessed be God, **The Affectionate One.**
		Blessed be the LORD, **The Embracer.**

Behaviors are contagious. Have you ever been next to a person who yawns, and you start to yawn? Have you ever heard someone in the room laughing and soon everyone is laughing? Behaviors like these allow us to participate in a primal physiological response that signifies a hidden communication within ourselves, a profound empathy with others, and a deep intimacy with God.

First, at one level, a yawn is a communication signal between the body/physical and the body/mental. The message is simple. Breathe deeply and fully. The yawn stimulates blood flow to the brain. It is designed biologically to communicate to the mind a basic need for oxygen in order to thrive. This is referred to as a body/mind connection.

Second, at another level, a yawn is an empathetic connection with others. It sets up a bond of nonverbal recognition or rapport. The message is more complex: I see you and breathe life with you. The yawn is one way that we identify with another person and share our basic need for one another to thrive. It is a system designed to recognize the affiliation we have for one another, sharing a life force that connects us to each other. This is sometimes referred to as a body/soul connection.

Third, at an additional level, a yawn is a deep intimacy with God. It takes us to the place of our creation when God formed humankind and gave us the breath of life. "And the LORD God formed man of the dust of the ground and breathed into his nostrils the breath of life; and man became a living soul" (Genesis 2:7). In other words, The Great I AM is as close to you as the breath of life itself. The yawn is an incarnational reality of God's Presence living within. It reminds us that we live and move and have our being in God. God is Breath. Breath is Life. Life is God. This is known as a pneumasomatic[40] or spirit/body connection.

A pneumasomatic connection through a contagious behavior points to Blessing God's Name when we reason by faith. An example follows:

```
Behavior ——> yawn

Original Intent ——> oxygenate

Instinctual Behavior ——> sucking (air)

God's Name ——> The Giver, The Nurturing One, The Breath of Life

Blessing Litany ——> Blessed are You, LORD God, The Giver.

                    Blessed be God, The Nurturing One.

                    Blessed be the LORD, Who is The Breath of Life.
```

Behaviors are habitual. Have you ever met with a friend for lunch on a weekly basis or called a family member each day? Have you ever brushed your teeth repeatedly two to three times a day? Behaviors like these allow us to establish routines that bring order to an ever-changing world. They provide regular touchstones that allow our stress to decrease and our ability to manage a fast-paced world to increase. Sometimes, these behaviors are unconscious. They are so automatic that we do not think about them. Breathing or praying to engender life are a few examples. Other times, these behaviors are conscious. We decide to add them to enhance the quality of our lives. Regular exercise or healthy eating are two examples.

Habitual behaviors, whether conscious or unconscious, can direct us to blessing God's Name when we practice Faith Listening. An example follows:

```
Behavior ——> exercise

Original Intent ——> to move

Instinctual Behavior ——> competition

God's Name ——> The Prime Mover, The Challenger, The Competitor, The One Who Participates.

Blessing Litany ——> Blessed are You, LORD God, The Prime Mover.

                    Blessed be God, The Challenger.

                    Blessed be the LORD, The One Who Participates.

                    Blessed are You LORD God, The Incarnate One.
```

Behaviors are addictive. Have you ever done something repeatedly and were powerless to stop doing it: drinking, smoking, or eating chocolate? Perhaps you stopped for a while, thinking you conquered the craving, but it returned in full force. Addictive behaviors can work for your benefit, or they can work for your harm. An addictive behavior such as exercise can be beneficial whereas an addictive behavior of promiscuous sex can be harmful. In any case, addictive behaviors have an original intent as well as an underlying instinctual behavior.

Addictive behaviors, when they are brought into the light of conscious reflection, can guide us to blessing God's Name. An example follows:

Behavior ———>	sex
Original Intent ———>	pleasure
Instinctual Behavior ———>	reproduction
God's Name ———>	The Creator, The Pleasurable One, The Desirable One, The Sensual One, The One Who Produces, The One Who Reproduces
Blessing Litany ———>	Blessed are You, LORD God, **The Creator.**
	Blessed be God, **The Pleasurable One, The Desirable One, The Sensual One.**
	Blessed be the LORD, **The One Who Produces.**
	Blessed are You, LORD God, **The One Who Reproduces.**

Whether a behavior is addictive, habitual, or contagious, it is possible to grasp Who God is by identifying God's Name. When we call upon God's Name, we are consumed no longer by the human behavior, but we are drawn closer into an intimate relationship with God who is "reconciling and making all things new" (2 Corinthians 5:17–20). And so, as we listen by faith and hold fast to our heart's desire, we learn to celebrate God's Presence acting in and among us.

C | CELEBRATE GOD'S PRESENCE

God gives us our heart's desire! What is yours? As you celebrate God's Presence, you may find that God is your heart's desire. All too often we forget God and place other people or things at the center of our lives. We get caught in a vortex of uncertainty and confusion instead of experiencing God's Peace that passes all understanding.[41] When behaviors are "beyond belief," there is a tendency to focus on the person, rather than on God. Behaviors provide an opportunity to come into God's Presence once you create a Blessing Litany and discover your Breath Prayer.

First, create a Blessing Litany. Let the behavior, the original intent, and the underlying instinctual behavior direct you to God's Name. Use word associations to find additional Names for God.

My Blessing Litany

The behavior is _____

The original intent is _____

The underlying structure is _____

Blessed are You, LORD God, _____

Blessed are You, LORD God, _____

Blessed are You, LORD God, _____

Blessed are You, LORD God, _____

Blessed are You, LORD God, _____

Blessed are You, LORD God, _____

Second, choose a Blessing Prayer. Read your Blessing Litany aloud. As you do so, inhale to "Blessed are You, LORD God," and exhale to "God's Name" for each Name you discovered. Say the Blessing Litany silently by using your breath to open your heart. Select one Blessing Statement that allows your breath to deepen and your muscles to relax.

My Blessing Prayer is

_____

Third, focus on God. Read your Blessing Prayer aloud three times by inhaling to "Blessed are You, LORD God," and exhaling to "God's Name." Say it silently to yourself three times.

Fourth, listen by Faith. Make some notes about what you are experiencing. Reflect upon your behavior in the light of celebrating God's Presence. Be sure to write down your physical sensations, emotional feelings, and mental thoughts.

REFLECTION NOTES ——————— ●

_____

_____

_____

_____

_____

_____

_____

Well done! You are on your way to develop your ABC skill of Faith Listening specific to a behavior. If you need further practice or are curious about another person's behavior, feel free to complete Practice Sheet 5| Chapter 5| The Body/Behavioral and the Intent of a Behavior. As you do so, remember that a behavior is the outward or inward expression generated by an emotion whose purpose is to deal with internal or external stimulus. First, the stimulus is perceived by the brain, which activates a sensory response in the body/physical. Second, this response energizes the body/physical for action, and the body/mental labels it as an emotion. Third, once the emotion is labeled, a behavior follows complete with an original intent and a basic human instinct for life. God is Life. Let your behavior be the catalyst for you to discern Who God is and What God is doing.

May God, The Active One, guide your every move!

Write a few statements about a behavior specific to an experience or a relationship. It might be your own or another person's behavior. Perhaps it is one that recurs or consumes you despite your best efforts. Whichever you choose, bear in mind that the human drama is set in the Story of God's Life. You are the living text of God's Word, just like in scripture. The key is to shift perspectives and listen to How God is actively present.

_____
_____
_____
_____
_____
_____
_____
_____

A | Awaken to God's Life

There are three ways to awaken to God's Life through a behavior: name, intent, and instinct. Let your behavior point you to a Name for God. If you are having difficulty identifying the intent or instinct, please review the discussion about both in Chapter 5.

① Behavior

Go directly by naming the behavior. Circle the behaviors in your story and choose one.

My behavior is _____

② Intent

Go foundationally by identifying the original intent of the behavior.

The original intent of the behavior is _____

③ Instinct

Go indirectly by identifying the human instinct of the behavior.

The human instinct of the behavior is _____

B | Bless God's Name

Discover how a behavior leads you to God's Name. Take a few deep breaths. Convert each discovery into God's Name. Generate more Names by using a thesaurus to find associated words.

Discoveries	**God's Name**
Behavior _____	_____
Intent _____	_____
Instinct _____	_____

C | Celebrate God's Presence

There are three ways to come into God's Presence. All draw on the ancient spiritual practice of blessing God. First, create your Blessing Litany. Second, read your Blessing Litany. Third, establish your Blessing Prayer which is a prayer of adoration.

① Create a Blessing Litany

Transfer the Names of God you discovered in B | Bless God's Name. Each one is a Blessing Statement in your Blessing Litany. Check to be sure there are no pronouns: I, me, mine, ours, or yours at the end of each Blessing Statement. A Blessing Litany is all about God.

> **Blessing Litany**
>
> Blessed are You, LORD God, The_____
>
> Blessed are You, LORD God, The_____
>
> Blessed are You, LORD God, The_____
>
> Blessed are You, LORD God, The One Who_____
>
> Blessed are You, LORD God, The One Who_____
>
> Blessed are You, LORD God, The One Who_____

② Read your Blessing Litany

Say your Blessing Litany aloud. Inhale when you say, "Blessed are You, LORD God," and exhale to "God's Name" for each Blessing Statement.

Repeat your Blessing Litany silently. Let your rhythmical breath guide you into celebrating God's Presence.

③ Establish your Blessing Prayer

Choose one Blessing Statement from the Blessing Litany that captures your attention or imagination.

Select one that deepens your breath or relaxes your muscles. Pick one that you like best or makes the most sense to you. Open yourself to the reality that God's Spirit, Pneuma, is in every breath you take. Remember: God is Life. Life is Breath. Breath is God.

> **Blessing Prayer**
>
> _____

Breathe your Blessing Prayer, a Prayer of Adoration, through your body. Repeat this prayer three times. Inhale when you say, "Blessed are You, LORD God," and exhale to "God's Name."

Reflect on Your Story

? What difference does it make when you allow your Body/Behavioral and the intent of the Behavior to embrace God Who is actively present for you?

? What happens when you identify Who God is, What God is doing, and How God is present in the context of your story?

? What new insights did you gain when you practiced Faith Listening to discern God's Presence?

Other Faith Listening Opportunities

☐ Create a Blessing Litany and a Blessing Prayer based on behaviors.
  → Take a piece of paper and make four columns.
  → Column 1: Write down a list of behaviors.
  → Column 2: Identify the intent of each behavior.
  → Column 3: Specify the instinct of the behavior.
  → Column 4: Name God.
  For example, the behavior is hair twisting. The intent is to sooth. The instinct is to grasp. God is The Weaver, God is The Comforter, and God is The One Who Holds.

☐ Select a friend's or family member's behavior that leaves you confused or wondering, "What were they thinking?" Apply the ABCs of Faith Listening to that behavior. After breathing the Blessing Prayer, send it forth by blessing the person. Say, "May You, LORD God, (God's Name) be so for (person's name)."

CHAPTER 6 | The Body/Spiritual and the Symbol of Dreams

· ·

For God speaks in one way, and in two …
in a dream, in a vision of the night … and with pain."[42]
—Job 33:1-33

What is the body/spiritual except the perceiver of God's Presence acting in creation and within the human being? The body/spiritual senses God's Breath living in and among us. It is here that each of us grasps God Who is Spirit when the wind sweeps over the face of the water … when life is being formed in the void[43] … when the Mystery of God's Action prevails in the darkness of the womb or tomb. Psalm 139 refers to the fact that dark and light are both alike to God and that we are knit together in our mother's womb, fearfully and wonderfully made. It is here in the darkness that the meaning of a life lived in covenant relationship with God is recorded, before it is made manifest in the body: physically, emotionally, mentally, behaviorally or spiritually. It is here at the very core of our existence that the intimacy of God's Relationship with us is made known before words are formed and meaning is assigned.

Elihu imparts a similar understanding to Job when he speaks of Who God is and How God communicates with us. This conversation between Elihu and Job is filled with wisdom. It provides insight into the Mystery of God's Life unfolding through the body/spiritual in the form of "a dream or a vision of the night when deep sleep falls upon mortals, while they slumber in their beds" (Job 33:15). Elihu stands on the very premise that "The Spirit of God has made me and the breath of the Almighty has given me life" (Job 33:4). He states, "God is greater than any mortal. Why do you contend against God saying, 'God will answer none of my words'?" (Job 33:12c-13). Some of us might even ask, "Where is God? Or why me?" It is God who "opens our ears, turns us from our despair and saves us from the Pit" (Job 33:16-18). Elihu knows that through a dream we can be reconciled to God and returned to God's saving embrace.

Dreams come to us in familiar form. We dream of what is familiar to us based on our human experience. A person, object, place, or action in a dream may be simply a literal representation, allowing you to process your daily life. Or, it may be a symbolic representation of a deeper connection with and communication from God. You may well wonder, "How is it possible to know the difference?" Let us begin to know the difference by reviewing the types of dreams found in scripture and by practicing the ABCs of Faith Listening.

Dreams come in one of six types: revelatory, visitation, prophetic, predictive, interpretative, and integrative. All encourage us to experience a deeper connection with God. Some provide direction and guidance. Others confirm a call or mission in the world. Each type of dream contains within it the reality that God is speaking. The key is to unlock the Mystery of God's Voice and discern God's Call to action through symbolic representations found in everyday life and informed by scripture from Genesis to Revelation. It is through dreams that come in the night or by day that God speaks. It is through dreams that the core of our being responds to God's Love working deeply within us.

1. **Revelatory Dream**

   A revelatory dream is an ecstatic expression or a mental sight in which something new is being revealed. It is a new understanding of God in picture form or auditory form such as an oracle—a divine utterance of words. It reveals God's Character or Nature.[44]

   Scripture

   After these things the word of the LORD came to Abram in a vision, saying, "Do not fear, Abram, I am a shield to you; your reward shall be very great" (Genesis 15:1).

   Real Life

   April, a thirty-eight-year-old woman, reported her dream. She said, "I was wrestling with a woman in a vast expanse of space. I saw myself duty bound to live out my role as a good wife and mother, but I was exhausted. I felt vocationally bound to live out my vow as an elder, but I was a failure. The woman pinned me to the ground, and I looked up. There, above me, I saw a figure clothed in radiant white, saying in a loud voice 'Well done, good and faithful servant!'"

   April's critical voice gave way to this new voice, relieving her of her ideals and perfectionism. She found a renewed sense of confidence and her energy returned. April was no longer bound to be perfect, but rather she was set free to live into a vibrant relationship with God.

2. **Visitation Dream**

   A visitation dream is a vision that occurs while asleep or awake. It is experienced as a glandular, visceral, or tangible reaction embodied in physical and emotional reality. It leaves an impression, and the mind wonders, "Is this real or not?" Only as life unfolds does the dreamer realize that the dream was real.[45]

   Scripture

   At Gibeon, the LORD appeared to Solomon in a dream by night; and God said, "Ask what I should give you." And Solomon said, "You have shown great and steadfast love to your servant my father David … Give your servant therefore an understanding mind to govern your people, able to discern between good and evil; for who can govern this your great people? It pleased the LORD that Solomon had asked this. God said to him, "Because you have asked this, and have not asked for yourself long life or riches, or for the life of your enemies, but have asked for yourself understanding to discern what is right, I now do according to your word. Indeed, I give you a wise and discerning mind; no one like you has been before you and no one like you shall arise after you. I give you also what you have not asked, both riches and honor all your life; no other king shall compare with you. If you will walk in my ways, keeping my statutes and my commandments, as your father David walked, then I will lengthen your life" (1 Kings 3:4–15).

Real Life

Megan, a seventy-one-year-old woman, recalls a dream that is as alive today as it was sixty-three years ago. At the age of eight, she heard her aunt say, "Your father is dead!" Meg replied, "No, he is not dead. He is alive!" Several days later, she fell asleep and dreamed. "I sensed a strange presence hovering over me. Suddenly, a bright light opened my eyes. I was transported to the river, accompanied by this angelic creature. Although everything inside of me wanted to cross over to the other side of the river, I was not allowed to do so. There, standing on the riverbank, I saw my daddy going about his business with others on the other side of the river. Although he had died few days earlier, I knew that he was alive and well. He, like the others, were tasked with a purpose and absorbed in their mission."

Megan realized that this dream had guided her throughout her life. Her relationships, educational pursuits, and career choices contained the thin veil between life and death. She knew beyond a shadow of doubt that resurrection was real and that life continued after death.

3. **Prophetic Dream**

A prophetic dream calls a people or a person into a right relationship with God. It recognizes that a covenant has been broken or that idols are being worshiped. It points to the fact that the people have gone astray and sets the crooked path straight.[46]

Scripture

Thus, the LORD God showed me, and behold, He was forming a locust-swarm when the spring crop began to sprout. And behold, the spring crop was after the king's mowing. And it came about, when it had finished eating the vegetation of the land, that I said, "LORD God, please pardon! How can Jacob stand, for he is small?" The LORD changed His mind about this. "It shall not be," said the LORD (Amos 7:1–9).

Real Life

Kimberly, a sixty-year-old woman, read a dream from her journal that had haunted her for several years. "I felt myself sinking into the mire of quicksand. It was dark all around me, and the landscape was barren. Struggling, I attempted to save myself. But, the more I struggled, the more I sank. Then, I heard a voice say, 'Be still!' I ceased to move, looked around, and there above me was a figure holding out a hand. I grasped the hand and was lifted onto a high pace and was set on solid ground."

Kimberly and I read Psalm 46:10: "Be still and know that I am God!" After meditating on this passage, she realized that in her willful independence and determination to make things right, she had relied on her own strength and had become her own god. The dream restored her faith and set Kimberly on a path to live into a dynamic relationship with God.

4. **Predictive Dream**

A predictive dream may point to something in the future or to someone beyond human experience. It provides a warning or gives a new direction.[47]

Scripture

Jacob came to a certain place and stayed the night. He dreamed that there was a ladder set up on the earth, the top approaching heaven; and the angels of God were ascending and descending on it. And the LORD stood beside him and said, "I am the LORD, the God of Abraham your father and the God of Isaac; the land on which you lie I will give to you and to your offspring; and your offspring shall be like the dust of the earth, and you shall spread abroad to the west and to the east and to the north and to the south and all the families of the earth shall be blessed in you and in your offspring. Know that I am with you and will keep you wherever you go, and will bring you back to this land, for I will not leave you until I have done what I have promised." Then Jacob woke from his sleep and said, "Surely the LORD is in this place and I did not know it." And he was afraid, and said, "How awesome is this place. This is none other than the house of God, and this is the gate of heaven" (Genesis 28:12–15).

Real Life

Samuel, a thirty-two-year-old man, was diagnosed with kidney failure. He had been sick for over a year and had tried a variety of traditional and nontraditional treatments. During this time, Samuel was filled with anxiety about his future and those of his family. He and his wife had one child and another on the way. One night he had a dream. "I saw myself lying on a dirt floor in Africa. It was dark, and nothing was familiar. There was a woman sitting beside me, chanting and spreading ointment on my body. A tingling sensation came over me, and I was healed."

Prior to his diagnosis, Samuel was instrumental in establishing a nonprofit organization to support a ministry in Africa. During one of his trips to Africa, elders of the church prayed for his healing. A year after his dream, he received a kidney transplant and is living a robust life with his wife and children. In addition, Samuel followed God's Call into a music ministry.

5. **Interpretive Dream**

An interpretive dream assigns meaning to people, places, or things based on a symbolic understanding. It looks at the dream from three perspectives: as a projection of the self, as a perception of another, and as a representation of a common topic.[48]

Scripture

Daniel sees a lion, a bear, a leopard, and another strange, ten-horned beast come out of the sea. The Ancient of Days judges the beasts, and the Son of Man is given dominion over all the earth. The four beasts represent human empires (Daniel 7:1–28).

Real Life

Mike, a thirty-year old man, shared his dream. "There was a mystic woman in black, sitting on a gravesite. A little boy was digging to get close to his parents. He wanted to follow in his parent's footsteps, but he could only write a name on the tombstone. It was St. Francis."

Mike realized that St. Francis's decision to turn from parental authority and affluence to God's Authority and Abundance was similar to his own. He said, "If St. Francis can do it, then I can too, with God by my side." This dream gave him the courage and an inner conviction to serve God, rather than please his parents.

6. **Integrative Dream**

An integrative dream takes fragments from everyday events or activities and puzzles them into a whole picture. It processes information from a person's daily life to give clarity and to find meaning.[49]

Scripture

The hand of the LORD was upon me, and He brought me out by the Spirit of the LORD and set me down in the middle of the valley; and it was full of bones. He caused me to pass among them round about, and behold, there were very many on the surface of the valley; and lo, they were very dry. He said to me, "Son of man, can these bones live?" And I answered, "O LORD God, You know" (Ezekiel 37:1–10).

Real Life

Bob, age forty-two, described his dream. "I dreamed that the patriarch was dying. I started praying immediately. I ran upstairs and found him dead. A figure appeared on a cloud, and I strummed my guitar. Then, the patriarch's left toe started to wiggle, and I woke up."

Bob, father of four, said that the day before he had been running up and down the stairs. The gout in his left toe was painful. He awoke to the fact that he was now the patriarch of his family. This dream gave him the clarity to pray more and play his guitar. Bob said that his dream provided him with "a sense of relief and comfort."

Remember, some dreams are a specific type: revelatory, visitation, prophetic, predictive, interpretative, or integrative. Other dreams are a combination of types such as those in Zechariah.[50] In other words, they can be understood from more than one perspective. The types are not cast in concrete. They are fluid. They offer a guiding principle to How God speaks to us through dreams.

The type or form of a dream may be insightful when determining the meaning of the dream, but it is not essential. Rather, it is essential to discern God's Name and grasp Who God is and What God is doing before assigning meaning to the dream. All too often, as we awaken to God's Life, we experience a sense of fear. That is, we stand on the cusp of awe and terror at the reality of God's Power and Majesty. When we bless God's Name and celebrate God's Presence, we discover that God has been with us all along. No matter how terrifying or exhilarating the dream is, we can be assured that God is with us.

A | AWAKEN TO GOD'S LIFE

We awaken to God's Life through our senses. Likewise, we awaken from a dream with sensory information that is coded in words, pictures, and sensations. Sometimes, we have an emotional reaction[51] or are moved to an action or behavior[52] because of a dream. Other times, the sense of smell and taste are triggered. These may be linked to experiential memories through the mind's eye.[53] In any case, following are examples of how to find Who God is and What God is doing through your dream by applying the ABCs of Faith Listening.

1. **Recall the Dream**

   Gloria, age thirty-six, had a dream that haunted her. When she told me her dream, she was visibly shaken. This is what she said, "Last night I woke up screaming. The dream was a dark one. There was a black ominous shape, sucking my soul out of me. I saw myself standing there in my pajamas with gray bottoms and a blue top. I also saw myself above the shape, looking down."

   Gloria informed me of the events that led up to her dream. She stated, "I am troubled by this dream because now I am in a loving relationship and plan to be married in eight months. Yesterday, I had several difficult conversations with others, regarding my past. I have spent the last seven years in a relationship in which I was unhappy and which drained the life from me. It ended last month through a divorce. I share joint custody for my six-year-old daughter with her father. These interactions bring up the past, and I end up exhausted from both my dreams and the conversations."

2. **Describe the Dream**

   At this point, I asked Gloria to think about the dream as if it were a plot, a story line, or a play. We began to unpack her dream by exploring several questions. Below are her responses.

   Q. What type of dream is it?
   A. visitation and integrative dream
   Q. Who is in it? (List all people and animals.)
   A. me
   Q. What is in it? (List all objects and things.)
   A. a black cloud
   Q. How did it happen? (List all actions.)
   A. screaming, sucking, standing, looking
   Q. Where did it happen? (List all locations.)
   A. earth and air
   Q. When did it occur? (List all time frames.)
   A. present

3. **Represent the Dream**

   Now, it was time for Gloria to explore her dream nonverbally. I gave her two pieces of blank, white paper. I asked her to represent her understanding of God on one and her dream on the other. Once she selected her medium of choice, chalk, she followed these simple instructions:

Represent your understanding of God on one piece of paper.

I instructed her to represent her image of God. I said, "Do not overthink it. Use your imagination. Trust your first response. If any words come to mind, write them on the back." I posed the following questions, and she created her God picture.

If God had a color, what color would God be for you?
If God had a shape, what shape would God be for you?
If God had a texture, what texture would God be for you?
If God had a movement, what movement would God be for you?
If God had a symbol, what symbol would that be for you?

Represent your dream on the other piece of paper.

I instructed her to use her imagination and create a dream picture. I told her that "your representation may be concrete and recognizable, or it may be abstract with swashes of colors and shapes with no recognizable figures or landscapes." She used colors, shapes, textures, movements, and symbols to draw her dream. She wrote her words on the back of the picture. This is what she drew.

God Picture

Dream Picture

B | BLESS GOD'S NAME

It is important to remember that human life is set in the context of God's Life. No matter what the dream, it can point us to God's Name and draw us into an amazing relationship with God. Gloria set out to discover how the dream was revealing God's Presence that she had missed in her description of the dream. Gloria became her own art critic. She unpacked her dream no longer from a human point of view, but from God's Life working through her.

Gloria listed the color, shape, texture, movement, and symbols she identified in each picture. Then, she named God based on her list. Gloria said she was surprised that she could come up with so many Names for God.

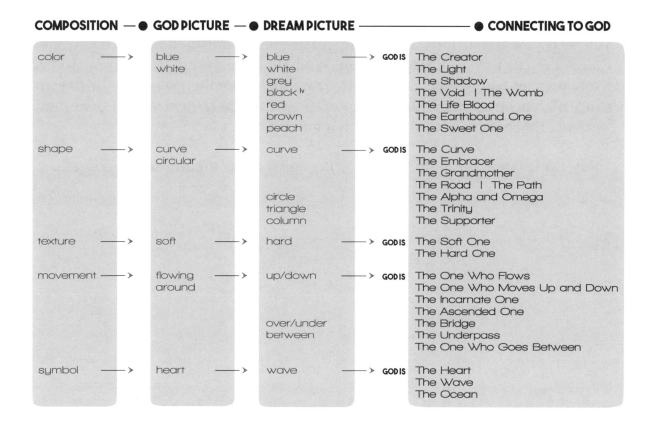

COMPOSITION —●	GOD PICTURE —●	DREAM PICTURE ——————————●		CONNECTING TO GOD
color →	blue white →	blue white grey black ᴵᵛ red brown peach →	GOD IS	The Creator The Light The Shadow The Void | The Womb The Life Blood The Earthbound One The Sweet One
shape →	curve circular →	curve circle triangle column →	GOD IS	The Curve The Embracer The Grandmother The Road | The Path The Alpha and Omega The Trinity The Supporter
texture →	soft →	hard →	GOD IS	The Soft One The Hard One
movement →	flowing around →	up/down over/under between →	GOD IS	The One Who Flows The One Who Moves Up and Down The Incarnate One The Ascended One The Bridge The Underpass The One Who Goes Between
symbol →	heart →	wave →	GOD IS	The Heart The Wave The Ocean

C | CELEBRATE GOD'S PRESENCE

Gloria created a Blessing Litany. First, she took the last column, and she wrote a Blessing Statement for each name: "Blessed are You, LORD God, _____." I said her Blessing Litany aloud for her while she listened. Together, we inhaled to "Blessed are You, LORD God," and exhaled to "God's Name" for each Blessing Statement. Second, Gloria selected one Blessing Statement that vibrated within. She chose the one that spoke to her. It was the one that allowed her to take a deep breath and relax the tension in her body. Third, she repeated the Blessing Prayer through her breath. Gloria inhaled to "Blessed are You, LORD God," and exhaled to "The Curve." She repeated this Blessing Prayer three times aloud and three times silently.

Gloria enjoyed being embraced by God as she reflected on her original dream. She reported that she could look at her dream and find new meaning. The shape was no longer dark and ominous, but rather it was a black curve out of which she had come. She realized that it was not her soul that was being sucked out of her, but rather her memories that had attached to her soul. Gloria breathed a sigh of relief as she embraced God's Presence, setting her free from her past and locating her on God's Path of Love.

There is much to learn from our dreams. Gloria provides one example. What is yours? If you are curious, follow the guidelines as outlined in Practice Guide 6| Chapter 6| The Body/Spiritual and the Symbol of Dreams. Discover How God is actively present with you, even when you dream. Remember, whether the dream is a beatific vision of an incredible experience or is a horrific drama of a human experience, both contain God's Life-Giving Presence.

May God, The Relational One, be your constant companion and friend!

Recall a dream. It may be a current dream or an old one. It could be a one time or reoccuring dream. It might be a pleasant dream or one that haunts you. Record your dream by writing about it.

_____

_____

_____

_____

_____

_____

_____

_____

_____

A | Awaken to God's Life

There are two ways to awaken to God's Life: evaluate and explore. Let's explore both.

Evaluate

Describe your dream. Think about it as a plot or story line in a play.

? What type of dream is it?

☐ **revelatory**   ☐ **visitation**   ☐ **prophetic**   ☐ **predictive**

☐ **interpretive**   ☐ **integrative**

? Who is in it? *List all people and animals.*

_____   _____

_____   _____

? What is in it? *List all objects and things.*

_____   _____

_____   _____

? How did it happen? *List all actions.*

_____   _____

_____   _____

? Where did it happen? *List all locations.*

☐ **earth**   ☐ **water**   ☐ **air**   ☐ **fire**   ☐ **other** _____

? When did it occur? *List all time frames.*

☐ **past**   ☐ **present**   ☐ **future**   ☐ **other** _____

Explore

Represent your understanding of God as you currently understand it. On a piece of white or black paper represent God. If God had a color, what color would God be? If God had a shape, what shape would God be? If God had a texture or movement, what would they be? Use crayons, colored pencils, chalk, or oil pastels. Choose colors, shapes, textures, movements, and symbols that best represent your image of God. Your God picture may be abstract or realistic. If words come to mind, turn your paper over and write the words on the back.

Represent your dream as it appeared to you. On a different piece of white or black paper express your dream. Use crayons, colored pencils, chalk, or oil pastels. Choose colors, shapes, textures, movements, and symbols that best represent your dream. Your dream picture may be abstract or realistic. If words come to mind, turn your paper over and write the words on the back.

B | Bless God's Name

There are two ways to bless God's Name: describe and review. First, use your artistic eye to describe what you see in each picture. Second, review similarities and differences in both pictures. Let's explore both.

Describe

List the colors, shapes, textures. and movements. Movements are the way your eye travels throughout the picture.

<table>
<tr><td>God Picture</td><td>Drean Picture</td></tr>
<tr><td>Color(s) _____
_____
_____</td><td>Color(s) _____
_____
_____</td></tr>
<tr><td>Shape(s) _____
_____
_____</td><td>Shape(s) _____
_____
_____</td></tr>
<tr><td>Texture(s) _____
_____</td><td>Texture(s) _____
_____</td></tr>
<tr><td>Movement(s) _____
_____</td><td>Movement(s) _____
_____</td></tr>
</table>

List the symbols in your pictures.

God Picture	Drean Picture
Symbol(s) _____ _____	Symbol(s) _____ _____

List any scripture that comes to mind.

Scripture _____	Scripture _____

Review

Evaluate your list by finding the similarities and differences. Circle the color(s), shape(s), texture(s), movement(s), and symbol(s) that are similar in both pictures. Then, underline the ones that are different in each picture.

Identify God's Name for each of the ones you circled and underlined. For example, the color red is associated with blood. Blood points to God's Name Who is Jesus, The Lamb of God, The One Who Sheds Blood, The Savior, and The Redeemer. For example, a circle is continuous, cyclical. God's Name is The Alpha and The Omega, The Beginning and The End.

	Similarities	**God's Name**
Color	_____	_____
Shape	_____	_____
Texture	_____	_____
Movement	_____	_____
Symbol	_____	_____
Additional	_____	_____
	_____	_____
	_____	_____

	Differences	**God's Name**
Color	_____	_____
Shape	_____	_____
Texture	_____	_____
Movement	_____	_____
Symbol	_____	_____
Additional	_____	_____
	_____	_____
	_____	_____

C | Celebrate God's Presence

There are three ways to come into God's Presence. All draw on the ancient spiritual practice of blessing God. First, create your Blessing Litany. Second, read aloud your Blessing Litany. Third, establish your Blessing Prayer which is a prayer of adoration.

 Create a Blessing Litany

Transfer the Names of God you discovered in B | Bless God's Name. Each one is a Blessing Statement in your Blessing Litany. Check to be sure there are no pronouns: I, me, mine, ours, or yours at the end of each Blessing Statement. A Blessing Litany is all about God.

Blessing Litany

Blessed are You, LORD God, The_____

Blessed are You, LORD God, The_____

Blessed are You, LORD God, The_____

Blessed are You, LORD God, The One Who_____

Blessed are You, LORD God, The One Who_____

Blessed are You, LORD God, The One Who_____

② Read your Blessing Litany

Say your Blessing Litany aloud. Inhale when you say, "Blessed are You, LORD God," and exhale to "God's Name" for each Blessing Statement.

Repeat your Blessing Litany silently. Let your rhythmical breath guide you into celebrating God's Presence.

③ Establish your Blessing Prayer

Choose one Blessing Statement from the Blessing Litany that captures your attention or imagination.

Select one that deepens your breath or relaxes your muscles. Pick one that you like best or makes the most sense to you. Open yourself to the reality that God's Spirit, Pneuma, is in every breath you take. Remember: God is Life. Life is Breath. Breath is God.

Blessing Prayer

_____

Breathe your Blessing Prayer, a Prayer of Adoration, through your body. Repeat this prayer three times. Inhale when you say, "Blessed are You, LORD God," and exhale to "God's Name."

Reflect on Your Dream

? What difference does it make when you allow your Body/Spiritual and the Symbols of Dreams to embrace God's Active Presence?

? What happens when you identify Who God is, What God is doing, and How God is present in the context of your dream?

? What new insights did you gain when you practiced Faith Listening to discern God's Presence?

Other Faith Listening Opportunities

☐ Keep a journal of your dreams. Choose any one and apply the ABCs of Faith Listening to discern How God is actively present for you in this dream.

☐ Invite a friend or family member to share a dream with you. Discern God's Presence by using the this Practice Guide. Option: You can use Practice Guide | Chapter 3, if the person is uncomfortable with artistic representation.

CONCLUSION | Discerning God's Presence

. . . .

"All things work together for the Glory of God."

—*Romans 8:28*

Faith Listening encourages us to discern God's Presence in our physical pain, our emotional turmoil, our mental anguish, our behavioral expression, and our spiritual distress. If we begin with the premise that we are formed in the image of God and are transformed by the mind of Christ, then we know that all things work together for good to the glory of God (Romans 8:28). Only then, do we awaken to the reality of Jesus's words: "The Kingdom of God is at hand (Luke 21:31) and "The Kingdom of God is within you ... among you" (Luke 17:21).

By now you have applied Faith Listening to your personal relationships and experiences. Some of you have explored the depth of your own soul to be reconciled to God and to be healed, finding wholeness of body, mind, and spirit. Others of you have practiced Faith Listening by hearing the stories of family, friends, colleagues, patients, and clients. Either way, these are two ways to apply Faith Listening. A third way is to apply it in a communal setting: a meeting, a faith community, and a family.

The communal application uses Faith Listening as a process to gather people together when conflict or disagreements arise. It offers an historical view based on What God is doing and How God is moving, rather than on who did what to whom, when and where. It focuses on issues and solutions, rather than on problems, personalities and behaviors. It provides an avenue to shift the paradigm from a human point of view to God's Perspective. It calls on people to hold sacred space for others while a diversity of voices are being heard. It creates a safe environment and reminds us that we live, move, and have our being together in God through the Body of Christ. Jesus is "the head of the body, the church ...For in him all the fullness of God was pleased to dwell, and through him God was pleased to reconcile to himself all things, whether on earth or in heaven (Colossians 1:18–20b). In other words, we can sing: "The fullness of the God-head bodily dwelleth in my soul ... And we are complete in Him."

In one case, a regional meeting of leaders from a variety of congregations gathered to discuss a national decision to ordain gay and lesbian priests. People came polarized on both sides of the issue and ready to defend their positions. Faith Listening was used as a process to hear all sides of the issue. Each person was invited to speak for no longer than two minutes. But, before speaking his/her own perspective, each person was asked to bless God's Name disclosed in the speech of the person who went before. A simple explanation was given to listen for the verbs used by the person and translate the action into God's Name.

For example, if a person repeated the phrase, "I am," then the blessing would be "Blessed are You, LORD God, the Great I AM!" Each person had the option, if they were unsure, to simply say: "Blessed are You, LORD God, The Mysterious One or The Unknown One." Only after God's Name was blessed could the speaker speak his/her viewpoint.

In another case, church members were divided between retaining or firing a much beloved music director. On the one hand, he had served the parish for ten years and was excellent at his profession. On the other hand, he had crossed over an ethical barrier with teenageers in the choir. Although the pastor was tasked with the hiring and firing of staff, she wanted to hear the diversity of opinions on the topic before making her final decision. To that end, an all-parish meeting was called. Faith Listening was used as a process to create a safe environment so that emotions and perspectives could be communicated with respect.

In both cases, an amazing thing happened. Civil discourse prevailed. Peace permeated the atmosphere. People felt that they were heard. The environment was enlivened by God's Presence as each person awakened to God's Life by blessing God's Name. And, in the great Jewish tradition, people argued for truth: not truth about who was right or wrong, but truth about Who God is and What God is doing. For if only God is Truth, then it is God Who is to be named in each encounter and in each experience. Brought alive was a group of people who in conflict and diversity found unity by blessing God's Name.

The purpose of Faith Listening is to find common ground in God. It is to remind us of the covenant relationship God holds with us in and through all experiences and relationships. For example, Rose and Bill disagreed about how to spend their money. Both had a valid point of view, but neither one could hear the other one's perspective. After a brief explanation of Faith Listening, Bill (the speaker) shared his perspective using an "I" statement: "I think it would be best to *purchase* a car." Rose (the listener) repeated the statement in Bill's exact words: "Bill, I heard you say it would be best to purchase a car." Then, Rose blessed the Name of God she heard in Bill's statement: "Blessed be the LORD God, Who is The Best One … The Wise One." Once Bill was heard, it was time for Rose to voice her perspective. Rose said: "I feel that it is more important to *buy* a washing machine." Bill parroted back her statement: "Rose, I hear you say that you feel it is more important to buy a washing machine." He too offered a Blessing Prayer: "Blessed be the LORD God, The One Who Feels or the One Who Touches." Together, they explored a common Name for God by choosing the verbs: *purchase* and *buy*. They settled into God's Presence by blessing God Who is The Buyer and The One Who Ransoms. Rose and Bill continued to discuss their finances, and they established a plan for purchasing both a washing machine and a car. They found a solution with God at the center. Rose and Bill moved from disagreement to agreement, from division to unity, by practicing Faith Listening.

Listening deeply to one another and discerning God's Presence is a powerful way to establish common ground and build unity. Faith Listening establishes a safe environment for people to be heard and to be reconciled to God. It is imperative that a process such as Faith Listening be applied when complaints, blaming, and chaos dominate the interaction in a communal setting: a family, an organization, a business, or a church. It provides a long-range view of How God is moving in and among us over a period of time, just like God moved with His people from Genesis to Revelation. This process is effective in reviewing the history of a faith community or an organization. If the human drama is in the foreground, then God's Story is in the background. By letting the background inform the foreground, an old meaning drops away, and a new meaning is revealed.

It is my hope that through the pages of this book you have learned the art of Faith Listening. Perhaps you discovered that Faith Listening creates safe environments and establishes sacred ground in which a diversity of voices can be heard and in which different perspectives can be respected. Maybe you explored Faith Listening as a communication process for both individual relationships and communal experiences. However you applied Faith Listening, know that it reconciles in times of conflict, engenders hope in times of despair, offers joy in the middle of suffering, and embraces peace in the face of conflict.

May God, The Compassionate One, walk with you,
lifting you when you fall and supporting you when you stand!

ADDENDUM A | Discovering God's Name

....

This chart is intended to be a reference guide only. It highlights a few of God's Names found in scripture with associated characteristics and attributes. *The Companion Bible, All the Divine Names and Titles of the Bible* by Lockyer, and *The 99 Beautiful Names of Allah* by Bawa Muhaiyaddeen offer additional names.

EL | The One and Only God
God in power and strength above and below, before and beyond all creation

Elohim	El-Elyon	El-Gibbor	El-Roi	El-Olam
The Creating One	The Most High One	The Mighty One	The Seeing One	The Eternal One
• Moves Creation • Plural in Unity Gen. 1:1,2b Jn. 1:1	• Dispenses Blessings • Divides Nations • Delivers Gen. 14:17-18 Ps. 97:9	• Pillar of Strength • Place of Protection Ps. 24:8 Ps. 57:2-3	• Reveals Truth • Visits Creation Gen. 16:13-14	• Establishes Security • Bridges TIme • Reveals Mystery Is. 63:16 Ps. 90:2

Eloah	El-Shaddai	El-Qanna	Ehyeh
The Adorable One	The Supplying One	The Jealous One The Passionate One	The Existing One
• Lives With • Rebuilds • Sanctifies Life Deut. 32:15-17 Job 19:25-26	• Gives Grace • Provides Need • Nurtures Gen. 17:1-8 II Cor. 6:18	• Enlives life • Shows Compassion Ex. 20:5 Joshua 24:19	• Self Identifies • Self Reveals • I am/was/will be(come) Ex. 3:13-15

Jehovah | I AM the LORD God
God in covenant relationship with and through all creation

Jehovah-Rohi	Jehovah-Hoseenu	Jehovah-Tsebaoth	Jehovah-Melek	Jehovah-Gmolah
• Shepherd Ps. 23:1	• Maker Ps. 95:6	• Lord of Hosts • Ruler 1 Sam. 1:3 Is. 6:3	• King • Enforcer Duet. 32:35-36 Jer. 38	• Recompense • Vengence Duet. 32:34-41 Proverbs 20:22

Jehovah-Shalom	Jehovah-Nissi	Jehovah-Shammah	Jehovah-Rophi	Jehovah-Jireh
• Brings Peace Judges 6:24 Ps. 23:2	• Banner • Victorious Song of Solmon 2:4 Is. 11:10-12 Ez. 17:15-16	• Is There • Presence Deut. 4:37 Ps. 139:4-12 Is. 63:9	• Heals • Mends Gen. 20:17 Ps. 103:3; 147:3	• Forsees • Provides Gen. 22:14

Jehovah-M'Kaddesh	Jehovah-Tsidkenu	Jehovah-Eloheka	Jehovah-Makkeh
• Sanctifies • Makes Holy Ex. 20:8-11; 31:13 Lev. 20:8; 21:7-8	• Makes Right • Judges Jer. 23:5-6; 33:16 Job 31:6	• Makes Covenants • Redeems Gen. 6:18; 9:16; 15;:18 Jer. 31:31	• Smites Ez. 7:9; 22:13 Malachi 4:6

Jesus | I am the...
God incarnate in and among all creation

Resurrection	Messiah	Christ	True Vine	Truth	Good Shepard
Jn. 11:25	Jn. 4:25-26	Jn. 15:1	Jn. 14:6	Jn. 10:11,14

Gate	Way	Light	Bread	Life
Jn. 10:7,9	Jn. 14:6	Jn. 8:12	Jn. 6:35	Jn. 11:25

The chart's primary function is to assist you in discovering God's Active Presence in daily life. Remembrance—anamnēsis—asks us to recall Who God is and What God is doing. This is an age-honored biblical tradition. The mandate to remember and call upon the Name of God occurs some 125 times in scripture.

The chart is a representation of God's Names as recorded in the Bible, the Torah, and the Koran. Not all names are included. You might discover additional names as you explore Who God is and What God is doing in the context of your daily life experiences and relationships.

The chart is designed for easy reference. It is organized in tiers, ranging from God Who is The Transcendent One to God Who is The Imminent One. It lists three classifications of God's Name. They are El Who is The One and Only God, Jehovah Who is The Relational God, and Jesus Who is The Incarnate God. It is to be noted that Adonai is a title, meaning the LORD Who is in relationship to the earth. It is equivalent to Jehovah.

The chart is simple to use. First, keep two basic assumptions in mind:

1. God is what God does.
2. The human being is formed in the image of God and transformed into the likeness of Christ.

Second, select an experience such as a physical pain, an emotional reaction, a mental obsession, a behavioral response, or a spiritual distress. You may want to select an event, a family dynamic, or a social/group issue. Ask yourself four basic questions to find God's Name:

1. Who is God?
2. What is God doing?
3. What aspect of God is being shown or Self-disclosed?
4. What aspect of God is missing or hidden?

Perhaps you selected the emotion of anger. Although the purpose of anger is to destroy the internal or external stimulus that threatens you, anger acts to motivate, to enliven life, to exact vengeance, or to make something right. When you realize that you are consumed by your anger and are acting out of instinct and self-preservation, ask yourself the four questions listed above. Use the chart as a reference guide. Here you will discover a variety of God's Names: El Kana Who Enlivens Life, Jehovah Gmolah Who is The Vengeful One, Jehovah Tstdkenu Who Makes Right, or Jesus Who is The Life. But, what if you do not find a corresponding Name? Then, be practical. If anger is your defense mechanism, then God is The Defender. If anger motivates you, then God is The Motivator. Focus on one Name for God. Choose the one that captures your imagination and allows you to breathe a sigh of relief. Take a deep breath. Inhale to "Blessed are You, LORD God," and exhale to "God's Name." Repeat this Blessing Prayer three to seven times. Ground yourself in the Presence of God. Connect with God. From this place of connection, what difference does it make? What new insight have you gained? How has God's Active Presence given you new meaning?

ADDENDUM B | Compassionate Listening

Compassionate Listening is another name for Faith Listening. Sometimes, a person is uncertain if God exists due to personal experiences that contradict religious dogma. It may be a person who claims to be an agnostic or an atheist. Other times, overt conversations about God are frowned upon. This may occur in workplaces such as businesses or nonprofit organizations. In both cases, the ABCs of Compassionate Listening is the preferred practice.

Compassion is a characteristic common to all caregivers. It is a value common to all spiritual traditions. Compassion draws its strength from the nature of what it means to be human. The primal instinct to care drives a person to act with passion in the face of suffering and pain. Compassionate Listening focuses on a person telling his/her story without the listener getting caught up in the storyteller's emotions or behaviors.

Compassion differs from empathy and sympathy. Empathy is a visceral response at the gut level. For example, a person yawns, and you do the same. A person feels pain, and you feel it in your body. Sympathy is an identification response at the mental or emotional level. For example, a person is out of work, and you feel sorry for him/her because you experienced a similar situation or can imagine what it is like to be without a job. Compassion is a relational response that calls for action. For example, a person is homebound, and you go to visit or arrange for food to be delivered.

Compassionate Listening is one action that finds its root in love. This love is unconditional, merciful, and hopeful. It is unconditional because the listener expects nothing in return from the speaker. It is merciful because the listener places no judgement on the speaker. It is hopeful because the listener connects the speaker to a life-giving experience.

Compassionate Listening focuses on one of two aspects of a person's story. They are need and value. Each one provides an opportunity to practice the ABCs of Compassionate Listening. Either one embraces a compassionate heart. Remember, first master the skill of Compassionate Listening by applying it to your own stories, and second, practice the skill by listening to another person.

1. **Identify the need**

    A. Awaken

    Be aware of the need. For example, if the person is anxious, the need may be *calm*. If you are not sure, ask the person or yourself, "What do you/I need right now?"

B. Breathe

First, couple your breath with your need. Inhale deeply. Exhale and speak the word *calm* aloud. Invite the person to join you. Inhale and exhale three times, saying the word *calm* each time you exhale. Second, let your breath carry calm through your body. Inhale deeply. Exhale and say the word *calm* silently to yourself at least three times on the exhale. Encourage the other person to do the same.

C. Center

Connect to the identified need, which is *calm*. As the mind goes, so the body goes. The body/brain knows how to be *calm* if you think *calm*. Keep focused on the word *calm*. Word has power. Pay attention to your physical sensation as you breathe *calm* through your body.

REFLECTIONS

What difference does it make? What new insights have you gained?

2. **Recognize the greatest value**

A. Awaken

Be aware of the greatest value. For example, a person may be worried about money. Money may be a symbol of worth, power, or security. Security is a value. If you are not sure what the value is, ask the person. "What does money represent to you? What benefit do you get from having money? What is your greatest value?"

B. Breathe

First, inhale deeply. Exhale and speak the word *security* aloud. Invite the person to join you. Inhale and exhale three times saying the word *security* as you exhale. Second, breathe *security* through your body. Inhale deeply. Say the word *security* silently to yourself at least three times on the exhale. Encourage the other person to do the same.

C. Center

Connect to the value of *security*. As the mind goes, so the body goes. The body/brain knows how to be secure when you think *security*. Keep focused on the word *security*. Word has power. Pay attention to your physical sensations as you breathe *security* through your body.

REFLECTIONS

What difference does it make? What new insights have you gained?

Compassionate Listening assumes that God supplies our every need and that God is the greatest value. It is the need or the value that points to God who reconciles and heals. Although you may connect the need identified or the value expressed with a Name for God, keep it to yourself. Compassionate Listening focuses on the worldview of the other person. If a person struggles with faith or is uncertain about God, then it is important to create a safe environment for that person to explore his/her understanding about the source of his/her life or the mystery of something or someone greater than the person. Let the need or value speak for itself in a way that makes sense to the other person. Conclude by saying to the person, "I wonder, what your experience of Compassionate Listening was?" Finish by offering a blessing to the other person by saying "May You, The Calm One, be so for (insert person's name)!"

ADDENDUM C | Making a Difference

. . . .

What people are saying about Faith Listening...

This skill of breathing and praying in the moment lets me relieve the stress of the moment.

The relationship between physiological and meditative techniques enriches my daily prayer.

This technique infuses the everyday with meaning.

This decreased my pain and gave me a new perspective on it. All of which I can take to the pulpit and preach it.

This day-to-day application by example is, to me, more useful than theory. I see God in more places which fosters hope.

It gives me the power of breathing, relaxation, and the ease of finding God in any situation. Now, I can look for God in more ways in my life.

I can be more attentive to the words of others and connect them to the presence of God.

This is a tool I can build on to bless God, be more prayerful, and understand God's presence in all situations.

It makes God right here and right now. My verb was "are" and my mantra this week will be "Blessed are you, Lord God, YOU ARE!"

Thank you for the possibilities.. that I can actually read scripture and use Faith Listening with my children.

This is a personal challenge to turn everyday situations and conversations into positive, God oriented experiences.

The possibility of encountering God in every blink and breath is real. I can touch the wonder and praise God through reworking a piece of scripture.

It is a practical communication skill that I can use with my spouse when conflict arises or disagreements occur.

I can look at Scripture as a blessing prayer. I am open to Scripture as insight into the fullness of who God is instead of what is it trying to tell me.

These are a few client comments that represent the difference Faith Listening made in their lives.

NOTES

INTRODUCTION

1. Genesis 1 and 2.

2. Pneumasomatic is a term that refers to the *Pneuma* or Spirit of God interacting with the *sōma* or body of a person. They are Greek terms Paul used to translate the Hebrew concept of *Ruâh* or Breath of God and *Nepesh* or living soul. "And the LORD God formed (hu)man of the dust of the ground, and breathed into his nostrils the breath of life; and (hu)man became a living soul (Genesis 2:7). It is to be noted that, in Hebrew, the body and soul are one. This wholistic concept was lost in translation from Hebrew to Greek. As a result, a split occurred and the body/physical was pitted against the body/spiritual. Faith Listening embraces the paradoxical nature of being human. The trichotomy of body, soul, and spirit are not separate, but one interacting with one another. It is this interaction that needs to inform our pastoral and health-care practices.

3. Covenant Theology. This theology is based on God's relational covenant with all creation as recorded from Genesis to Revelation. Scripture, read from a Covenant perspective, gives insight into the Self-revelation of God's Name and Character. It provides an interpretive grid to grasp the Mystery of God's Presence moving with, in, and among us from generation to generation. There are five basic covenants God makes with humankind through leaders. They are with Noah (Genesis 9:15-18), with Abraham (Genesis 27:1-10, Exodus 2:24), with Moses (Exodus 34: 27-28), with Jeremiah (Jeremiah 31:31, Hebrews 8:8), and with Jesus (Hebrews 12:24).

4. Formation Theology. This theology is based on the scriptures that we are "formed in the image of God" (Genesis 1:27) and transformed by the mind of Christ. "Let this mind be in you that is in Christ Jesus" (Philippians 2:5). "Be transformed by the renewing of your mind" (Romans 12:2b) for "we have the mind of Christ" (1 Corinthians 2:16b). God forms us in our mother's womb where "we are fearfully and wonderfully made" (Psalm 139:14b).

5. Body Theology. This theology is based on the incarnational reality of God in the life, death, and resurrection of Jesus. The Hebrew worldview accepts the paradoxical nature of God being both transcendent and immanent. Unlike the Greek worldview of spiritual and physical duality, the Hebrew worldview recognizes the intimate interaction between the two as one because no life exists without God. Paul attempts to explain this when he describes resurrection (1 Corinthians 15) and uses the body and its members to clarify the Gifts of the Spirit (1 Corinthians 12). Ashley provides a comprehensive overview of Body Theology in *Theologies of the Body: Humanist and Christian*.

6. Anamnēsis is a Greek term that means remembrance. It assumes the active Presence of God as we recall God's Actions and bless God's Name. It is a spiritual practice that focuses on remembering God. Unlike amnesia, when we forget God and remember only the human experience, anamnesis implies that God's Presence is with us. It occurs each time we come together before the altar in worship and celebrate the Eucharist. It is calling, into the now, the reality of what has gone before and what will come again. God is The Alpha and The Omega (Revelation 1:8), the beginning and the end, The One Who Was and Is and Evermore Shall Be.

7. "I will bless the LORD at all times" (Psalm 34:1). "Pray without ceasing" (1 Thessalonians 5:17).

CHAPTER 1

8. Psalm 34:1–3; 103:1, 2, 22; 113:1–3; 135:19–21; 145:1–2.

9. *The Companion Bible* focuses on God's Names as revealed in scripture. Lockyer provides a comprehensive review in *All the Divine Names and Titles in the Bible*.

10. See Addendum A for an overview and chart of the Names of God both Jewish and Christian.

11. Bawa Muhaiyaddeen cites *The 99 Beautiful Names of Allāh* in the Muslim tradition.

12. God's Name was too sacred to be spoken, according to the Hebrew people. By 300 BC, the unpronounced Name for God was translated into a tetragrammaton, YHWH, meaning Yahweh, or JHVH, meaning Jehovah. This serves as a silent mantra, inhaling to YH (Yah pronounced ya-Hey) and exhaling to WH (Weh pronounced Va-Hey). In the third century, Hebrews ceased using Yahweh and replaced it with Elohim, a plural understanding of God who is sovereign above all gods. Between the sixth and tenth century, as Hebrew was translated into Latin, Y was replaced with J, and Jehovah, meaning brings into existence, became a well-known Name for God. Addendum A provides a chart that offers an overview of God's Names.

13. Lockyer lists God's Names and their meanings in two books: *All the Men of the Bible* and *All the Women of the Bible*.

14. Emmanuel is a Hebrew Name for God, meaning God is with us.

CHAPTER 2

15. Romans 8:1–39, specifically Romans 8:22.

16. Grace provides a detailed explanation of this interpretive grid in "*Living Epistles: A Pastoral Response to People in Pain*."

17. Brand and Yancey developed the concept of "theological words pregnant with theological meaning" in *Fearfully and Wonderfully Made*.

18. See Addendum A. El Shammah is a Hebrew Name for God, meaning God is there.

19. Phillips suggests in *Your God Is Too Small* that our understanding of God is limited for modern times and encourages the reader to grasp a wider perspective of God.

20. James introduced the Name of God as "The More" in *The Varieties of Religious Experience*, 394–402.

21. Pelletier describes autogenic training in *Mind as Healer, Mind as Slayer*. Autogenic training is a desensitization-relaxation strategy developed by Johannes Heinrich Schultz in 1932.

22. Autton offers an overview of hypnosis in *Pain: An Exploration*.

23. Bandler and Grinder describe Neurolinguistic Programming (NLP) in *Transformations: Neurolinguistic Programing and the Structure of Hypnosis*. NLP is a systematic model of communication that uses the power of words to reprogram the neurological system for the purpose of processing information, changing behaviors and beliefs, and reframing meaning.

24. Benson deepens the relaxation response by utilizing "The Faith Factor" as described in *American Health*, May 1984, 48–53. The Faith Factor asks a person to focus on his/her breath for one to three minutes. And, with each exhale, to say the word "one" or a word that best represents a faith value such as love. Research shows that this has significant health benefits.

CHAPTER 3

25. Harmony with God and humility before others is best described in *The Interpreter's One Volume Commentary on the Bible*, 849–50.

26. Jesus heals a woman—Matthew 9:20-22; Mark 5:25-34; Luke 8:43-48. Jesus prays in the Garden of Gethsemane—Matthew 26:39; Mark 14:36; Luke 22:42.

27. Revelation 1:8-11; 21:6; 22:13.

28. See Addendum B for a description of Compassionate Listening.

29. Young, R. *Analytical Concordance of the Bible*. Peabody: Hendrickson Publishers. Note: This concordance is "designed to lead the simplest reader to a more correct understanding of the common English Bible, by a reference to the original words in Hebrew and Greek."

30. 2 Corinthians 3:2-3.

CHAPTER 4

31. Chapter 2 describes how physical sensations point to God's Name. When you label your emotion and locate its corresponding physical sensation, your will become more aware of God's Active Presence in your life. Naming God allows you to bless God's Name in the context of everyday life, including traumatic and joyful situations.

32. Chapter 3 describes how a mental cue (a verb or action) points to God's Name. As you describe your emotion, pay attention to the verbs you use. Both lead you to the reality of God's Presence embodied within and suggest a Name for God.

33. Names of God that use an emotional descriptor of God's nature include the following:
    · God is an angry God—Mark 11:15.
    · God is a jealous God—Exodus 20:5, 34:14; Deuteronomy 4:4, 5:9, 6:15; Joshua 24:19.
    · God is a vengeful God—Deuteronomy 32:35; Psalm 94:1; Isaiah 35:4, 61:2; Romans 12:19; Hebrews 10:30.
    · God is a loving God—I John 4:8, 16.

34. Robert Plutchik (1927-2006) was a psychologist, an adjunct professor at the University of South Florida, and a professor emeritus at the Albert Einstein College of Medicine. After receiving his PhD from Columbia University, he authored or coauthored more than 260 articles, forty-five chapters and eight books. He edited seven books. His research focused on the study of emotions, the study of suicide and violence, and the study of the psychotherapeutic process.

35. Panentheism means "all-in-God" and refers to the Ancient Greek πᾶν *pân*, "all", ἐν *en*, "in" and Θεός *Theós*, "God." It is a worldview in which all creation is good; it recognizes Jesus's proclamation that the Kingdom of God is near, at hand, and within; it acknowledges that God is with and in us. God is everywhere, Omnipresent. God's Divine Presence permeates and penetrates every part of life, including the universe and beyond through space and time. Panentheism is to be distinguished from Pantheism. Pantheism means "all is God." It maintains that the divine and the universe are one. That is, God is the tree or rock. Panentheism makes a distinction between the divine and the universe. That is, the rock is a symbolic object that points to and participates in God's Life Who is The Creator of the Universe. Panentheism is most pronounced in Celtic Christianity, Creative Spirituality, and Mystical traditions.

36. See divine actions of the Jealous God in Joshua 24:1-28. God's divine jealous actions are both harsh and loving. God is the Law Giver as described in the Mosaic Covenant and the Lover as described in Jesus's summary of the Law

(Mathew 22:36-40). On the one hand, God punishes. God is the Judge. God is the Consuming Fire (Deuteronomy 4:24; Hebrews 12:29). God is the Vengeful One. His wrath and anger is quenched with mercy when he is reminded of His Covenant with Moses or His Covenant Promise with Noah. On the other hand, God is Love (1 John 4:8, 16). He cares for His people like a mother hen cares for her young.

CHAPTER 5

37. Original intent of a behavior refers to the first time the behavior is expressed. It is possible to change an unwanted behavior by identifying the original intent. Simply generate behavioral options by brainstorming those that satisfy the original intent. Select the one that makes the most sense; check for internal objections to the new behavior; adjust accordingly and make an agreement to change. Although this sounds simple, it is complex because some behaviors have a secondary gain. In other words, someone or some part of you benefits from continuing the unwanted behavior. Suffice it to say that this is one way to make behavioral changes. The other way is to practice the ABCs of Faith Listening by linking the original intent with God's Name. Behavioral change is a natural outcome of Faith Listening.

38. Spink, 35-42.

39. Primal instinctual behaviors are hardwired into the human brain for survival purposes. They are innate and emerge without any training or education. Instinctual behaviors are different from reflexive behaviors. Reflexive behaviors are physiological in nature such as pupils contracting to decrease the amount of light hitting the retina.

40. Pneumasomatic connections are those that integrate spirit and body. *Pneuma* is an example of a biological word pregnant with theological meaning as discussed in Chapter 2. The word *Pneuma* in Greek refers both to God's Spirit and to physical lungs. Other examples might include the heart with the symbolic meaning of God's Love.

41. A Benedictine Blessing recited at the end of Eucharist in the Episcopal Liturgy reads: "May the Peace that passes all understanding keep your hearts and minds in the knowledge of Jesus Christ, Our LORD" (John14:27).

CHAPTER 6

42. Chapter 2 explores a way to discern God's Presence through pain.

43. Void. The void in Hebrew means without form, where space is dark and black. Like the deepest space of the cosmos or the creative space of the womb, life is hidden from view. Life is unseen, unheard, and unknown. God's Mystery of creation is yet to be revealed. Dark and black take on new meaning in light

of God's Action. Some of us have equated dark and black to ominous and evil forces that cause us to live in fear and terror. Others of us have embraced dark and black as the place of awe and wonder to await the discovery of God's re-creation, forming us anew. Brown, in her book *Learning to Walk in the Darkness*, provides further insight into the spiritual practice of walking in the darkness.

44. Revelatory dreams in scripture include Isaiah 6:1-8; Daniel 2:19; Acts 7:30-32, 9:3-6.

45. Visitation dreams in scripture include Genesis 32:23-26, 46:2; Exodus 3:2-3; Job 4:13-16; Luke 24:1-51; 2 Corinthians 12:1-4; Acts 10:3.

46. Prophetic dreams in scripture include Amos 8:1-6, 9:1.

47. Predictive dreams in scripture include Daniel 2:28, 4:5; Matthew 2:12-13, 27:19; Acts 9:10-11, 16:9, 18:9, 22:18, 27:23.

48. Interpretive dreams in scripture include Genesis 41:1-7; Judges 7:13-15; Acts 10:9-17; Revelation 1:12.

49. Integrative dreams in scripture include Ezekiel 1:4-14, 8:2.

50. Combination of different forms in scripture include Zechariah 1:8, 3:1, 4:2, 5:2, 6:1.

51. Chapter 4 discusses a process to discern God's Presence through emotions.

52. Chapter 5 outlines a way to discern God's Presence through behaviors.

53. The sense of smell and taste can trigger associated memory experiences. For example, the smell of roses may remind you of your grandmother, because she used rose-scented perfume. You smelled the scent of roses each time she hugged you,. The dream may or may not be understood as the Wisdom of God coming forth or speaking to you in the familiar form of your grandmother.

54. Black is the absence of color, according to color theory. Things are black until light exists. The human eye cannot distinguish color or texture without light. The artistic eye awaits the mystery of light to break forth and specify a color. Black is neither good nor bad. It is value neutral until light reveals its color.

REFERENCES

· ·

Armstrong, Karen. *The Case for God.* New York: Knoff, 2009.

Autton, Norman. *Pain: An Exploration.* London: Darton, Longman & Tood. 1986.

Bandler, Richard and Grinder, John. *Transformations: Neurolinguistic Programing and the Structure of Hypnosis.* Moab: Real People Press, 1981.

Bawa Muhaiyaddeen, M.R. *The 99 Beautiful Name of Allāh.* Philadelphia: The Fellowship Press, 1979.

Benson, Herbert. *The Faith Factor.* American Health. May, 1984, p. 48-53.

Benson, Herbert. *The Relaxation Response.* New York: Avon Books, 1975.

Brand, Paul and Yancey, Phillip. *Fearfully and Wonderfully Made.* Grand Rapids: Zondervan, 1980.

Brand, Paul and Yancey, Phillip. *In His Image.* Grand Rapids: Zondervan, 1984.

Brown, Barbara Taylor. *Learning to Walk in the Darkness.* New York: Harper One: 2015.

Grace, Jo Anne. "Living Epistles: A Pastoral Response to People in Pain", *Journal for Health Care Chaplaincy,* 1994.

Grace, Jo Anne. "Pneumasomatic Care™: A Ministry of Reconciliation and Healing", *The Journal of Christian Healing,* Spring/Summer, Vol.24, Number 1. 2008.

Holy Bible, New Revised Standard Version. New York: Oxford University Press, 1989.

James, William. *The Varieties of Religious Experience.* New York: Collier, 1961.

Lockyer, Herbert. *All the Divine Names and Titles in the Bible.* Grand Rapids: Lamplighter Books, 1975.

Lockyer, Herbert. *All the Men of the Bible.* Grand Rapids: Lamplighter Books, 1968.

Lockyer, Herbert. *All the Women of the Bible.* Grand Rapids: Lamplighter Books, 1968.

O'Donohue, John. *To Bless the Space Between Us.* New York: Doubleday, 2008

Pelletier, Kenneth. *Mind as Healer, Mind as Slayer.* New York: Delta. 1977.

Phillips, J.B. *Your God is Too Small.* New York: Collier Books, MacMillian Publishing Company, 1961.

Plutchik, Robert. *The Emotions,* Revised Addition. Lanham: University Press of America, 1991.

Rupp, Joyce. *Fragments of our Ancient Name.* Notre Dame: Sorin Books, Green Press Initiative, 2011.

Sasso, Sandy Eisenberg. *In God's Name.* Woodstock: Jewish Light Publishing, 1994.

Siirala, Aarne. *The Voice of Illness: A Study in Therapy and Prophecy.* Philadelphia: Fortress Press, 1964.

Spink, Amanda. *Information Behavior: An Evolutionary Instinct.* Berlin: Springer, p.35-42, 2010.

The Companion Bible, King James Version. Grand Rapids: Kregel Publications, 1990

The Interpreter's One Volume Commentary on the Bible. Nashville: Abingdon Press, 1971.

Young, R. *Analytical Concordance of the Bible.* Peabody: Hendrickson Publishers, 1984.

ABOUT THE AUTHOR

Jo Anne Grace, Ph.D. is a pastoral theologian, a spiritual director, a hospice chaplain, and a health educator. Her private practice focuses on Pneumasomatic Care™ ... a ministry of reconciliation and healing. This ministry integrates Spirit and body to bridge the gap between theology and physiology, between faith and health. Dr. Grace specializes in brain health to counteract the effects of stress, trauma, and compassion fatigue. She connects physical reality with spiritual certainty by teaching people practical skills to move through their pain and fear. Jo Anne lives in Steamboat Springs, Colorado, where she attends St. Paul's Episcopal Church.

You can contact Dr. Grace at joannegrace.psc@gmail.com and visit her website at joanne-grace.com.